# The Hegartys
# of the Laurels

## A Story of Unsung Heroism

Jim Hegarty

The Hegartys of The Laurels

A Story of Unsung Heroism

by Jim Hegarty

Copyright ©2021 Jim Hegarty

ALL RIGHTS RESERVED

ISBN: 978-1-914488-32-0

Including the right of reproduction in whole
or in part in any form.

This edition printed and bound in the Republic of Ireland by

lettertec

Lettertec Publishing

Springhill House,

Carrigtwohill

Co. Cork

Republic of Ireland

www.selfpublishbooks.ie

Cover design by John Joseph Hegarty.

*Dedicated*

*To all of those who have gone before us*

*and left such a legacy*

*All Primary Resources are available on*

*www.hegartycollection.ie*

# Foreword

Jim Hegarty has been a friend for many years and a neighbour of my late parents Ruairí Brugha and Máire MacSwiney Brugha. I always hoped that he would write a history of his family's role in Ireland's struggle for freedom and independence.

In this memoir, Jim shows how their family at 'The Laurels' on the Pouladuff Road worked together during the War of Independence. His story is warm, illuminating, fascinating, and it gives an excellent insight into the period in Cork. Hopefully, this story will encourage others to write their stories of our struggle for freedom.

In 2020, we had the centenary of the assassination of Tomás Mac Curtáin, after serving only two months as Lord Mayor of Cork. It was also the centenary of the death on hunger strike of his successor, my mother's father, Terence MacSwiney. He had a vision to undermine the corrupt and corrupting British Empire. He was an optimist, a pragmatist, an idealist, and an opportunist. Britain's arrest of him provided the opportunity. During his court-martial, he wore his Lord Mayor's chain, and in effect, he turned the tables on the court, declaring them illegal. Then started the global campaign to weaken the grip that the empire had in Ireland, that eventually would weaken it elsewhere.

During 2020, we were proud of MacSwiney's intelligence, his vision, and his achievements, but my thoughts constantly went to the eleven who continued on hunger strike in Cork Gaol in solidarity with him. And then to Michael Fitzgerald, who already had health issues when he started his hunger strike and died after 67 days. When the great leader Liam Lynch was dying during the tragic civil war, he asked to be buried alongside Michael Fitzgerald. Joseph Murphy died the same day as Terence MacSwiney, after 76 days on hunger strike. Jim's father, John Joe Hegarty, was close to Joseph Murphy. In his memoir, Jim reveals that Joseph had been engaged to Mary O'Leary, who later married Timothy (Taedy) Owens. Her granddaughter Máire Owens is married to my brother Terry.

In March 1963, John Joe Hegarty was one of those who organised the erection of a monument to his fallen republican comrades buried in St. Finbarr's Cemetery.

President Eamon De Valera travelled to Cork to officially unveil it on St. Patrick's day. The night before, there was a bomb explosion, which was intended to be under the platform where the speakers were to be the next day. One of those involved died, and another was seriously injured. My parents and I were due to be on that platform! Another connection with my friend Jim Hegarty that I hadn't known until he wrote his memoir!

Reading it, I am reminded of bringing my parents to see a certain well-known film and listening to my mother speaking through the film: 'Well, that never happened!' And my comment on the way out: 'A good movie, but the truth was much more exciting.' Jim's memoir captures the excitement of those times.

My vision is of transition year secondary school students throughout Ireland being asked to do a project that would capture many more of these stories. They then could be held in history departments in colleges, as was done for folklore, in the thirties. The folklore collection gathered by primary schools is held in UCD and is a fascinating resource. Over these years, I have promoted a process of Recollect-Reflect-Reconcile and Inspire.

Jim Hegarty's account does precisely this and is an example for others to follow.


Prof. Cathal MacSwiney Brugha
March 2021

# Contents

# Introduction

From a young age, I knew my father, John Joe Hegarty, had played a role in the War of Independence and the Civil War. However, he never spoke to any of his children in any great detail of his or his siblings' involvement. It came to the fore in my mind in 1960 as a ten-year-old when I saw him on parade along with many of his old comrades wearing their distinctive hats at our neighbour's house. This was on the occasion of a plaque being unveiled to the memory of Joe Murphy, a fellow volunteer, who had died on hunger strike in Cork Jail in 1920.

I had, over later years, made numerous attempts to piece together his story, not only from him but also from his sister Joanna (Nan), when she spent a lot of time at our home 'The Laurels' and from his comrades on their many visits to the house.

# The Laurels

'The Laurels,' with its market gardens and adjoining shop, was not only home to the Hegarty family, but it also served in its time, as a safe house for men on the run, a bomb and landmine factory, an arms store, an ammunition dump, an intelligence hub, and a Brigade office.

# Military Records

Over the years, I have built up a collection of primary material, including details relating to the funerals of Joe Murphy, Tomás Mac Curtain, and other Cork volunteers at the republican plot in Saint Finbarr's Cemetery Glasheen Cork. When the military records were released, it gave me a great insight into John Joe's activities and, just as important, those of his two sisters Mary Francis (Mamie) and Johana (Nan).

Their papers have also allowed me to write about and further research their family's personal history, a legacy to both their memory and their place in Cork's history in the fight for independence. Their story highlights the crucial role of women, not only in gun-running but their importance to intelligence gathering in any conflict. Their story is a testament to the courage and bravery of the women of Cumann na mBan.

Many books have been published about this period of our history, but there must also be a huge amount of family stories still unwritten. I hope my story will inspire or influence others to write about their family's involvement in this period of Irish history.

John Joe 1956

# John Joe Hegarty 1897-1973

My father, John Joe Hegarty, died on 6th June 1973. As an officer in the Old IRA 'H' Company 2nd Battalion 1st Cork Brigade, he was given a full military funeral at the family grave in St Joseph's Cemetery Tory Top Road, Ballyphehane, Cork. His funeral drew a large attendance of family, neighbours and friends. Many of his surviving Old IRA comrades, and a big contingent from the greyhound industry also attended to pay their respects.

When the prayers and oration were completed, a volley of shots was fired over the family grave by the military army before the playing of the last post; the tricolour was removed, and the burial commenced. As the youngest of his family and nearest to the firing party, I picked up the shells, at which point I was told by the army officer in command to leave them, as he had to account for them back at the barracks. A voice coming from behind me said, 'Leave the lad alone, that is his father.' When I looked around, I recognised the voice and face of General Tom Barry, who was a good friend of my father and one of his old comrades.

Barry was commander of the 3rd West Cork Flying Column and led many ambushes and reprisals during the War of Independence, and played a leading role in the anti-Treaty side during the Civil War. He was also a hero of mine from that time and had

previously given me a copy of his book *Guerilla Days in Ireland*.[1] As a result of his timely intervention, I was able to keep the shells, and they are still a prized possession of mine.

The Shells

WAR of INDEPENDENCE    1916 — 1923
CERTIFICATE of MERITORIOUS SERVICE

THIS is to Certify

*John Joseph Hegarty*

was a member of                    H        Coy.

2ND Batt.,              Cork No. 1 Brigade

Irish Republican Army

SIGNED    *Tomás Crofts*

*Michael Murphy* Brigade Officers.

PERIOD ......... to ...........

unit 59

Certificate of Service

1    (ISBN 9781781171714)

9789

Mr Rooney

The Laurel
Poulaudff Rd
Cork

Oct 17 1936

The Secretary
Office of the Referee
Griffith Barracks
South Circular Rd
Dublin

Ref. No 9789

A chara.

I am enclosing herewith further
additional evidence in connection with my claim
for a Service Certificate

Mise le meas

J. J. Hegarty

~ 4 ~

# New Ireland Assurance Company

When I was leaving the cemetery, I was approached by a staff member of New Ireland Assurance Company who asked me to call to his office on the South Mall on my return to work the following Monday. At that time, I was working with The Standard Life Assurance Company, a job incidentally my father arranged with the help of his friend Mr Dan Dineen from his greyhound connections in the Pouladuff and Bishopstown Coursing Club.

When I called to their office, I was handed an envelope containing a cheque to bring home to my mother. On enquiring whether they needed a death certificate, I was told, 'we know your father is dead, now bring the cheque home to your mother'.

I discovered later that prior to independence in 1921, there was only one Irish-owned insurance company, New Ireland Assurance, which was established in 1918 by entrepreneurs within the Irish Volunteers. On reflection, I am now of the belief that they were looking after one of their own regardless of whether he had an insurance policy with them or not. Many of their agents nationwide were, in fact, former volunteers. Whenever I subsequently met any of his former comrades, I felt they always wanted to make sure my family and I were getting on okay with our lives.

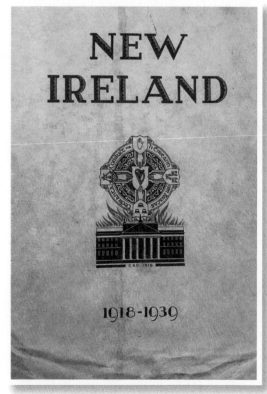

Early history of New Ireland

# Conn Neenan

One, in particular, Conn Neenan, a leading officer in the 2nd Battalion of the 1st Cork Brigade and prominent member of my GAA Club St.Finbarr's, always inquired when we met in the club about my career prospects as well as my social life. Conn even offered to lend me money to buy a house when I was getting married. This was in 1974, when mortgages at that time were very difficult to obtain, but I didn't need to accept his generous offer as I had a staff mortgage facility.

During my many chats with Conn about the War of Independence and the Civil War period either at the club or at his home, 'Fatima' on College Road, usually over a drink, in his case Remy Martin, he always spoke of his great respect for the role played by John Joe, Nan, and Mamie, but also always mentioning the role of both of my grandparents, Patrick and Elizabeth. He had dealt with them during that time as he was no stranger to 'The Laurels' and to the activities they were engaged in. He never went into any great detail, always finishing with 'you should be very proud of them, Jimmy, and stay out of harm's way'.

He wrote to me on one occasion about history being written. "Many who wrote history were very often taken by their own pens and distorted facts with personal praise.' Naming a number of such authors, he always finished with, 'my family were never guilty of that'. In penning this narrative of my family's story, his words have always resonated with me.

I was just 22 years of age when my father passed away at the age of 76 years, so as an adult, I did not have a great opportunity to share much time with him. I was, however, always aware while growing that he had a presence. I knew he and my mother had a reputation for being honourable and fair in their dealings in business, with people, and especially with family. I never heard either raise his or her voice in anger. In fact, growing up as their son felt like a badge of honour.

Tel. 41757

**Fatima,**

**College Road,**

**Cork.**

Friday.

Dear Jimmie:

1 am returning the papers you gave me, newspapers
like the Westmeath Independent might publish same but not any Pub-
lisher. No sale for suvh a book.

Many who wrote history were very often taken
by their own pens and distorted facts with personal praise.

O'Callaghan had two books. (This man is listed as British Agent)
Easter Lily and the killing of Mrs Lindsay. (disguting)

Pat Coogan. General errors.

Sean Neeson. Passing of mick Collins.

Seamus Malone Ford. all offer the beam.

Taylor on the killing of Sir Henry Wilson. By publishing a letter
from a well known Insurance man here which as a fake. Taylor
never wrote again.

Others too.
Brian Ingles On Casement.

All the best

Con

Con Neenan letter

# Silence is Golden

Like so many others, John Joe was reluctant to speak about his involvement as a young man within the IRA during the War of Independence and the subsequent Civil War. I remember asking him on a number of occasions about this period, and his stock answer was always the same, 'Florrie O'Donoghue (1st Cork Brigade Intelligence Officer) will explain it all in detail with his writings.' Yes, there has been a lot written about this period but so much more left unwritten. This is what I wish to address vis a vis *The Hegartys of the Laurels: A Story of Unsung Heroism.*

I always felt that his reluctance to speak openly was twofold: he did not want any bitterness to prevail; his children should treat people as they found them and not get involved with any republican organisations of the time.

Many decades later, having accessed military records pertaining to him and his sisters, I am now attempting to put on record the Hegarty's very deep involvement in the struggle for independence, as they risked their own lives and those of their parents.

# Pouladuff Road or Poll Dubh

The Hegarty home 'The Laurels' and its grounds were situated on the Pouladuff Road (Poll Dubh). The road is approximately one and a quarter miles in length and was a main road to Kinsale up until the 1960s. The area got its name from the time of public hangings and burials at Gallows Green at the city end of the road, the area now known as Greenmount. It is reported that members of the United Irishmen captured after the 1798 rebellion were hanged at Gallows Green, and it had been used as a place of execution for centuries. It should come as no surprise that the area became known as a dark place or black hole.

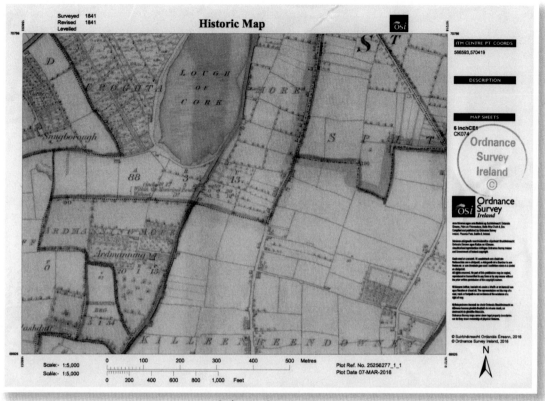

Ordnance Survey map

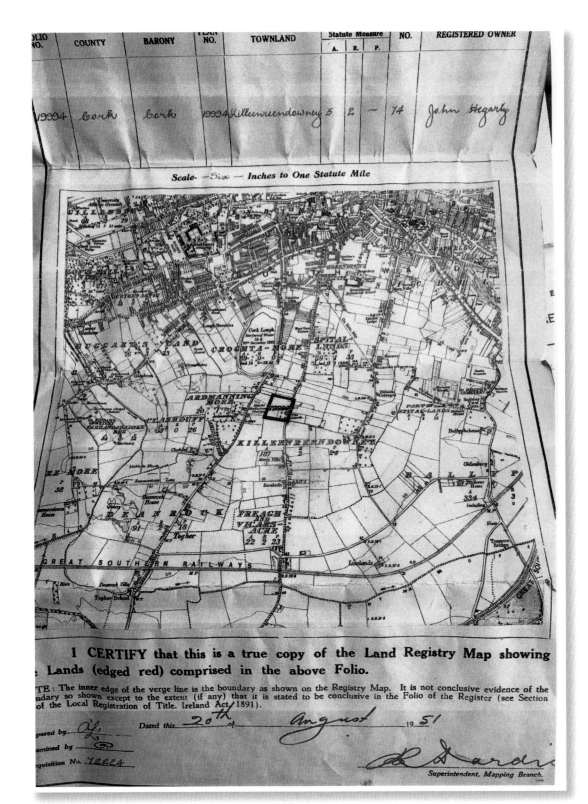

Maps

# DESCRIPTION OF LANDS.

PART of the Lands of    Killeenreendowney ----

containing    Three----      acres and two----     roods and perches or thereabouts statute measure situate in the Electoral Division of   Bishopstown--- Barony of   Cork---      and County of Cork..

The registration of the ownership of these lands does not extend to the mines or minerals therein the same being subject to the provisions in that behalf of the Irish Land Act, 1903.

~~The sporting rights within the meaning of the said Act to which the Vendor entitled exclusive of the tenant previously to the sale under the said Act are reserved.~~

# BURDENS.

The Lands above described are subject to :—

An annuity of   Eight---     pounds   five---     shillings and   two---     pence beginning on the 1st of   June 19 17--    and payable half-yearly to the Irish Land Commission until an advance of £ 254---      has been repaid.

NOTE :—These lands are registered subject to the rights or equities (if any) arising from the interest vested in   Patrick Hegarty by Fiat of the said Commission, dated the   25th.    of   January      19 17 , being deemed to be a graft on his previous interest in the land or arising in any other manner from the existence of such previous interest.

ate of Sir Charles
Piggott, Bart.
4874
15543

Registration

# Market Gardens

Pouladuff Road is on the south side of Cork city. This area and its surrounding areas, such as Togher and the area now known as Ballyphehane, were predominantly inhabited by market gardeners and their families. This is confirmed in the first available Ordnance Survey map of 1841. The Hegarty family were part of this community for many generations, until 1977 when they sold the property. As with all market gardeners at the time, they were self-sufficient, growing vegetables and fruit and also selling them daily at the city markets. It was also common for families to rear their own poultry and pigs. Many would have reared horses, both for working the land and for transport, and as such many of them had small blacksmith forges.

# Great Famine

John Joe's grandparents Patrick and Mary lived through the famine, and his parents all witnessed its devastating consequences for the country in its aftermath. As market gardeners, their circumstances and skills proved to be life-saving during this horrendous period in Ireland's history. The years between the 1840s and 1850s proved to be a period of mass starvation and disease. Evictions were in the region of 70,000, resulting in the displacement of up to 500,000 people. These evictions were caused mainly by absentee landlords looking to maximise their profits by converting from tillage farming to cattle grazing lands and thereby ridding themselves of their smallholding tenants. The nation's overall population decreased by up to 25%, resulting in over one million deaths and forced emigration. Some, such as John Mitchell, claimed the British authorities' policy was one of extermination, while others believed that there was no deliberate intention of mass killings on their part. The fact that there was sufficient food on the island at the time fuelled the existing hatred of colonialism. This would not be the last action or inaction of the British authorities in increasing the call for Irish independence from its empire. Either way, it had the effect of galvanizing support for nationalists. The Hegartys, along with many other local market gardeners, survived this terrible ordeal.

# Hegarty Lands

The Hegarty holding on the Pouladuff Road situated in the townland of Killeenreendowney, in the Electoral Division of Bishopstown and Barony of Cork, Folio 19994, was three acres and two roods. They had the use of additional fields, both on the Pouladuff Road itself, such as Lynch's and Sullivan's fields, and also on the Hangdog Road (now the Tramore Road).

The family story of the Hangdog Road was that it was built to facilitate Captain Sarsfield's family from Togher on their way to Sunday service in Douglas. On the first Sunday after completion, their journey was interrupted when they saw a dead dog hanging from a tree. This family of landowners played a significant role in the Hegarty's story during the War of Independence.

The 'Laurels' itself was built in the 1800s as a two-story house. The gravel was drawn from the nearby Tramore river. Some granite steps were also found there. The holding also included two small cottages, which were inhabited by local families (Carrolls and Ellises) up until the early sixties. The earliest family papers I have is the will of my great grandfather, Patrick Hegarty, dated 1885, bequeathing the ground to his son, my grandfather Patrick, and providing all of the other children with just one shilling each. The law of the land at that time did not allow a will to be contested if one inherited a shilling.

This resulted in all my grandfather's siblings emigrating to America over a period of time. He also made provisions for his wife Mary that in the event of him predeceasing her, she would continue to live at 'The Laurels'. In the event of her not getting on with her son Patrick, she was to be paid three shillings a week. Patrick inherited the holdings in 1917.

# This is the last Will and Testament

of me _Patrick Hegarty_ _____, of
_Killeenreendowney_, in the County of _Cork_
_Market Gardener_ _____, * made this
_twelfth_ day of _December_, in the year of our
Lord, One Thousand Eight Hundred and _Eighty five_

* Profession or Occupation.

**I hereby** revoke all other Wills and codicils heretofore made or purporting
to have been made by me. I appoint _____,
_____, of _____
in the County of _____, *
and _____
of _____, in the County of _____
_____,* to be Executors of this, my Will. I direct that
all my just Debts and Funeral and Testamentary Expenses shall be paid in the first
instance as soon as possible after my decease.

**I do hereby give and bequeath** unto _My Son Patrick_
_Hegarty My Ground House and Chattles._
_My Wife to live and be supported by my Son_
_Patrick as long as they agree together. And_
_Should they not agree to have my Son_
_Patrick pay My Wife Mary Hegarty Three_
_Shillings per week during her life —_
_And to my Children Michael, Margaret. Eliza,_
_Mary Anne, Julia, Ellen, and Hannah One_
_Shilling Stg. each —_

_Signed with my consent before_ } _Patrick X Hegarty_
_the Witnesses hereto named_ } his mark
_Witness Francis Cotterel_
_Jery Spillane_
_James Crowley_

_Decr 12th 1885_

Family Will 1885

# Hegarty Family

It was into this Roman Catholic family of Patrick Hegarty, a market gardener, and Elizabeth Hegarty (nee Walsh) that my father, John Joe Hegarty was born, on 25th September 1897.

The 1901 census has him living at 'The Laurels' as a four-year-old with both his parents, Patrick aged thirty-eight, Elizabeth aged thirty-six, their children Patrick aged twelve, Mary Frances (Mamie) aged eight, Johana (Nan) aged two, and a cousin, Lizzie O'Leary, aged twenty-one.

Both parents could read and write and spoke Irish as well as English. His brother Patrick, eight years older, about whom very little is known, died in tragic circumstances. The 1911 census has all the family still living at 'The Laurels,' with their cousin no longer resident, but there is a servant, a Ms. Archer. All the children attended their local National School in Togher, a path I would also take.

John Joe with his parents Patrick and Elizabeth, Grandmother Walsh and sisters Nan and Mamie c 1908

As with many families of that period, the parents and grandparents, the Hegartys and the Walshes from Grenagh living in Killingly were very much influenced by nationalism and were infused with the desire for the independence of Ireland from Britain. The Hegarty's were supporters of their local Cork MP, Charles Stewart Parnell, in his quest for land reforms and independence. Parnell was the first leader of the Home Rule Party and later the Irish Parliamentary Party.

Patrick carried on his watch fob Parnell's commemorative medal (Johnson), which had a shamrock and maple leaf on the central panel, with a side profile of Parnell and a border inscription that read 'Ireland's Army of Independence 1891'. The reverse is inscribed with 'Let my love be conveyed to my colleagues and the Irish people.' This is not surprising, as they were, after all, children of the famine era. They encouraged all their children to believe in and strive for Irish freedom, resulting in 'The Laurels' being regularly raided by the Royal Irish Constabulary (RIC), whose barracks was situated on the nearby Togher Road, and also by the British Army prior to the Easter Rising of 1916. These raids subsequently increased tenfold in later years during both the War of Independence and the Civil War.

Parnell Medal

Parnell Medal

Census Years / 1901 / Cork / Bishopstown / Killeenreendowney West / Residents of a house

**Residents of a house 5 in Killeenreendowney West (Bishopstown, Cork)**

✅ Show all information

| Surname | Forename | Age | Sex | Relation to head | Religion | Birthplace | Occupation | Literacy | Irish Languag |
|---------|----------|-----|-----|------------------|----------|------------|------------|----------|---------------|
| Hegarty | Patrick | 38 | Male | Head of Family | R Catholic | Co Cork | Market Gardener | Read and write | Irish and English |
| Hegarty | Elizabeth | 36 | Female | Wife | R Catholic | Co Cork | - | Read and write | Irish and English |
| Hegarty | Patrick | 12 | Male | Son | R Catholic | Co Cork | Scholar | Read and write | English |
| Hegarty | Manie | 8 | Female | Daughter | R Catholic | Co Cork | Scholar | Read and write | English |
| Hegarty | John J O | 4 | Male | Son | R Catholic | Co Cork | Scholar | Cannot read | English |
| Hegarty | Johana | 2 | Female | Daughter | R Catholic | Co Cork | Scholar | Cannot read | English |
| O leary | Lizzie | 21 | Female | Niece | R Catholic | City Cork | Scholar | Read and write | English |

# Pastimes

As a boy and young man living in the outer suburbs of the city, John Joe's interests focused mainly on hurling and football in St. Finbarr's club (Barrs) and road bowling on the Pouladuff Road itself. He was also involved with the local Cork National Hunt Club with members of his family, including his father Patrick, who was a founding member in 1880. The name of the club epitomised their nationalist beliefs and proved to be a constant reminder of their beliefs.

# Greyhounds

Later in life, breeding greyhounds became one of his passions, enjoying both open and closed coursing and also track racing. He became a founding member of the Cork County Open Coursing Clubs' Association and was on its committee, where he represented the Pouladuff and Bishopstown Coursing Club. His pride and joy was a dog that raced under the name of 'Hi Maeve', winning numerous races on the track and coursing events for him. 'Urhan Bridge,' another dog he bred at one time, held the 550-yard record at Youghal track. This gave him a great sense of satisfaction and pride. He later sold it to American breeders, who kept him informed of his progress.

Cork National Hunt Club c 1916. (John Joe sitting 3rd from the left)

Open Coursing Trophy Presentation to John Joe with his daughter Anne O'Driscoll, son Jack and Jack's wife Carmel

# Cork Volunteers

With the establishment of the Volunteers in Cork, like many young men in their twenties and younger, he joined and became immediately active. Both his sisters Nan and Mamie joined Cumann na mBan when it was established in Cork. They were all young volunteers helping to raise funds by collecting money at church gates around Cork city. They all became involved in training in the use of weapons at which they excelled. They organised military parades, drills and marches, and attended meetings in the Volunteers' headquarters on Sheares Street.

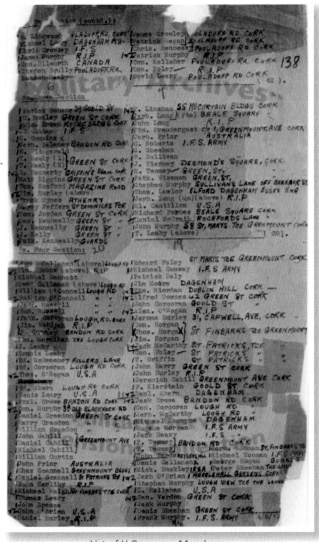

List of H Company Members

Copy of Company Register of Former "H" Company, 2nd
Battalion, Cork I Brigade - as compiled in Year 1921.
-----------------

Dan Murphy                Captain. **137**  See R.O/16?

Edward Barrett            1st Lieut (formerly Acted as Captain).

Thomas Leahy              2nd Lieut.

Con. O'Callaghan          Sect. Commdr. (No. 1 Section)

John J. Hegarty           do.       (No. 2 Section)

Tim. Hurley               do.       (No. 3 Section)

Jerh. Callanan            do.       (No. 4 Section) -formerly
                          acted as 1st Lieutenant.

Co. Quartermaster     Tim. Hobbs.(lieu Jerh. Long)        1964

Co. Adjutant          Owen Callanan.

st active at date
nd do                 **9**

No. One Section.

| | |
|---|---|
| Edward Barrett (above) BALLYPEHANE | Maurice Sexton, DOUGHCLOYNE, Cork |
| Thos. Murphy POULADUFF, RD, CORK | John Collins c/o QUEENS OLD CASTLE |
| 1+2 Jerh. Murphy POULADUFF, RD, CORK | Tim. Donovan USA |
| M. Hennessy POULADUFF, RD, CORK | Harry Lane, TOGHER, CROSS, CORK |
| 1+2 Tim. Ahern LEHENAGH, CORK, | Harry Harvey TOGHER, RD, CORK |
| J. Donovan LEHENAGH, CORK, | 1+2 J. Buckley U.S.A |
| J. Moran FAIRYVILLE LOUGH RD CORK | J. Sullivan U.S.A |
| 1+2 . Walsh LEHENAGHMORE Co CORK | Lm. Sexton TOGHER, RD CORK |
| A. Walsh LEHENAGHMORE Co CORK | M. Buckley TOGHER, RD CORK |
| J. Jackson ELFORD, DAGENHAM, ESSEX, Eng | Jerh. Crowley |
| Lar. Hurley ASHGROVE Co CORK | X Willo Regan TOGHER, RD, CORK |
| John Hurley CAPWELL RD CORK | M. Cronin TOGHER, RD, CORK |
| Patk. Hurley OLIVER PLUNKET ST CORK | Jerh. J. Murphy KINSALE RD CORK |
| Patk. Healy U.S.A | M. Coveney KNOCKLASHEEN CORK |
| M. Lonergan DOUGLAS Co CORK | D. O'Leary TOGHER, RD, CORK |
| D. Lonergan DOUGLAS Co CORK | J. Coveney R.I.P |
| J. Ryan QUARRY LANE CORK | D. O'Sullivan U.S.A |
| David Sheehan POULADUFF, RD, CORK | 1+2 Dan. Feeney TOGHER, RD, CORK |
| 1+2 Con. O'Callaghan (above) U.S.A | John Crowley TOGHER RD CORK |
| 1+2 Jerh. O'Connor TOGHER, RD, CORK | D. Murphy TOGHER RD CORK |
| Dan. Mullane | Thos. Collins HOLLYVILLE CURRA |
| Jerh. Mullane LEHENAGH Co CORK | 1+2 Chas. Harvey U.S.A |
| Jos. O'Callaghan LEHENAGH Co CORK | 1+2 Con. Regan 33, DUBLIN ST CORK |
| Dan. Coveney BLARNEY Co CORK | Sean Scanlon |
| Willie Harvey THE COTTAGE, GLASHEEN, RD | Son. Leahy R.I.P |
| Son. Manning R.I.P | Tim. O'Connor R.I.P |
| J. Brady TOGHER RD CORK | Jim Neill LEHENAGH CORK 55 |
| Chas. Feeney HIBERNIAN BLDGS CORK | |
| **28** | **27** |

No. Two Section.

| | |
|---|---|
| 2 Daniel Murphy (above) G.S.RLY ATHLONE | John Kelleher POULADUFF RD CORK |
| 2 John J. Hegarty (above) POULADUFF, RD, | Michael Lyons R.I.P |
| 2 Jas. Hennessy GEORGES QUAY CORK | John Murphy LEHENAGHBEG Co CORK |
| Jerh O'Leary U.S.A | John Torney GLASHEEN RD CORK |
| Patrick Desmond POULADUFF RD CORK | Jeremiah Scully POULADUFF R |
| Thomas Dooley POULADUFF RD CORK | James Crowley POULADUFF RD |
| John Harrington POULADUFF RD CORK | Daniel O'Connell POULADUFF R |
| Cornelius Harrington POULADUFF RD CORK | Patrick Crowley R.I.P |
| 2 Daniel Dempsey YOUGHAL MENTAL HOPITAL | Jerh. Desmond R.I.P |
| John Sheehan POULADUFF RD CORK | Michael Flaherty POULADUFF R |
| Jeremiah Fitzgerald POULADUFF RD CORK | Patrick Mahony BALLYPHEANE |
| Con. Fitzgerald U.S.A 55 | William Donovan DESMOND T |
| James Sheehan POULADUFF, RD, CORK | Michael O'Keeffe POULADUFF R |
| John Anthony ⎫ HIBERNIAN BLDGS CORK | (over) |
| Harry Anthony ⎭ | |
| **15** | **13** |

List of H Company Members

# 1918 Conscription Act

The Conscription Act for Ireland was passed by the British House of Commons on 16th April 1918.

Many young Irish men had been encouraged by John Redmond and his Irish Parliamentary Party to voluntarily join the British Army in their war effort. They did in their thousands, including one of my grandfathers, Patrick Allen (Royal Artillery). Many joined for altruistic reasons, fighting for the freedom of small nations, others for pure financial gain in order to support their families. Many prominent employers such as Guinness also encouraged their workers to join the war effort. They in fact offered to continue to pay 50% of their wages if they joined, and promised to keep their jobs for them.. All were promised a short war.

It must also be acknowledged that many, on returning home from war as fully trained and combat-hardened soldiers, joined the Volunteers. Men such as Tom Barry brought a professional training approach to the campaign in the fight for Irish freedom. Meanwhile, the leaders of the Volunteers were totally opposed to men joining any British regiment.

# Army Regiment

The passing of the Act saw the Hegartys fundraising for the Brigade to prevent the conscription of men into the British army during the First World War. This campaign was successful as conscription was never enacted in Ireland, unlike in the rest of the British Isles. There was an influx of young men joining the Volunteers while the threat of conscription existed, but once the British government abandoned this policy, their numbers dropped.

Those who left had used the Volunteers with the sole intention of avoiding conscription. On the other hand, John Joe and all his family were fully committed to the overall cause, honouring their oath and continuing their membership.

Meanwhile, since 1915 the government had been providing a grant to those who got a qualification in first-aid. Both Hegarty sisters under a Dr. Saunders and a nurse Miss Elwood, a fellow Cumann na mBan member, qualified firstly in order that they could attend to injured or wounded volunteers if and when required and secondly to use the grant money to bolster the Brigade funds. This was all in plain sight of the authorities they were working against. The knowledge they gained was put to good use and practice over the coming years of conflict, particularly the War of Independence and the Civil War that were yet to come. All three siblings were to become intelligence officers during the War of Independence and Civil War campaigns.

Recruiting office Patrick St (credit Cork Examiner)

# Westminster General Election, 1918

The family also involved themselves in national and local politics, an interest that sustained them for the rest of their lives and one which they passed on to their families.

Their first national campaign experience came on Saturday the 14th December 1918 when the United Kingdom general election was called after the armistice with Germany, which ended the First World War. Their various contributions included canvassing, distributing leaflets, erecting posters around the city, and assisting the Sinn Fein candidates standing for the Cork city constituency in the all-island Westminster elections.

Many Volunteers were on duty guarding the polling stations, ably assisted by Cumann na mBan members, who provided them with meals and refreshments.

Of the 105 Irish seats available nationwide, Sinn Féin won a total of 73 seats, and as a result of this support, they set up the first Dáil in Dublin in opposition and rejected the Westminster Parliament. Both Cork Sinn Féin candidates were elected with large majorities in their two-seater constituency.

The successful candidates were: J.J.Walsh, who fought in the GPO in 1916. He helped to found the Volunteers in Cork and was very active in the Gaelic Athletic Association (GAA). He took the Treaty-side in the Civil War and served as a minister in the first Free State government. On his demise, he left a fund to have a monument erected at the republican plot, which came to pass in 1963.

Liam deRoiste, who was chairman of the first-ever Sinn Féin meeting held in Cork and a founder of the Cork branch of the Gaelic League. He was a close friend of both Tomas Mac Curtain and Terence MacSwiney; both men were to be elected Lord Mayors of Cork, and both died at the hands of the British establishment while holding office.

This result also heralded the demise of John Redmond's Irish Parliamentary Party. This political party had encouraged thousands of Irish men to enlist in the British Army during the First World War in the hope that Home Rule would eventually be granted to Ireland.

In the constituency of Dublin St Patrick's, Countess Markievicz, a veteran of the 1916 Easter Rising, was elected as the first woman to the Westminster Parliament. As with all Sinn Féin MPs since then, she did not take up her seat in London. She resigned from Sinn Féin and became a Fianna Fáil TD when that party was established in1926.

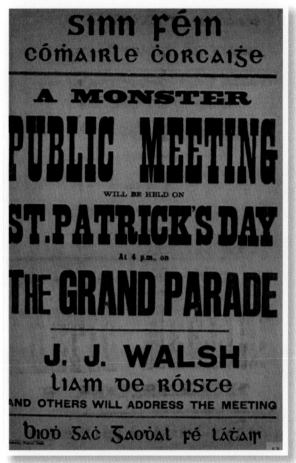

Countess Markievicz

1918 Election Poster

# Nan and Mamie's Role in Cumann na mBan

Nan became a captain and was also appointed treasurer to the Cork District Council at their AGM in the City Hall in 1920, a position she held until the disbanding of the organisation in 1925. Nan was also at this time carrying rifles and ammunition through the city for Capt. James Walsh, O.C. 9th Battalion.

Mamie was also responsible for establishing a number of branches within Cumann na mBan in Cork city, where she was a president. She also established further branches in Lehenaghmore in Togher, Ballygarvan, and at the seaside town of Ballycotton in East Cork. She carried guns and ammunition around the city, at times in a pram, for volunteers, and, similarly to Nan, she also brought despatches to the different branches. Jerry O'Brien, who was a member of the Active Service Unit (ASU), and an intelligence officer in 'H" Company, wrote that she carried a grenade for him after an operation, that he stayed in her home 'The Laurels', and that she assisted him by monitoring enemy agents around the greater Pouladuff area. In June 1921, Jerry was arrested with other members of the unit when they met in Stenson's public house on Douglas Street. He was subsequently released without any charges levelled against him.

Nan also did similar work carrying arms regularly for Mick Carey and other very active Brigade officers in 'G' Company, such as Conn Neenan and Sean Mitchell. Mitchell had her crossing the city during curfew hours, avoiding detection from the armed authorities. She continued this dangerous activity for the rest of the war, putting her young life at risk. Many 'H' and 'G' Company members were living and working in and around the Lough parish.

Jeremiah Keating, the intelligence officer of 'G' Company, who worked at Phairs on the Bandon Road, operated an arms dump on the premises and worked closely with John Joe, Nan, and Mamie. The shop provided excellent cover as it did not arouse suspicions from the authorities or spies when volunteers visited.

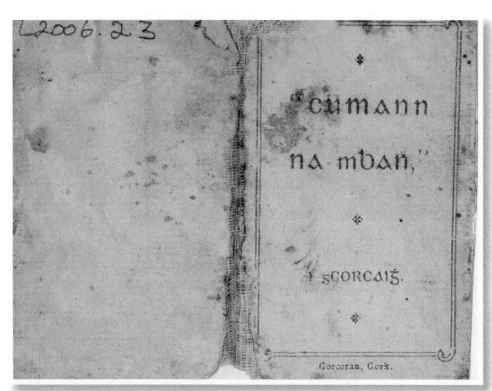

Mamie Cumann na mBan membership

Mamie Cumann na mBan membership

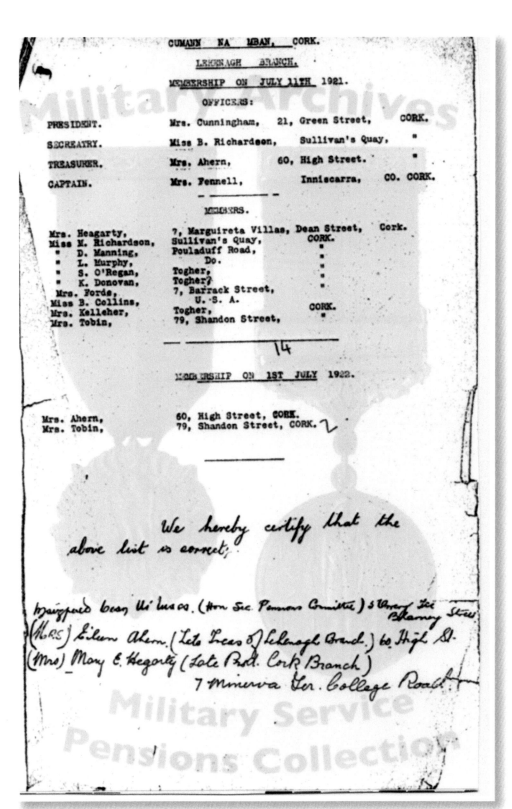

CUMANN NA MBAN, CORK.

LEENAGH BRANCH.

MEMBERSHIP ON JULY 11TH 1921.

OFFICERS:

| | | | |
|---|---|---|---|
| PRESIDENT. | Mrs. Cunningham, | 21, Green Street, | CORK. |
| SECREATRY. | Miss B. Richardson, | Sullivan's Quay, | " |
| TREASURER. | Mrs. Ahern, | 60, High Street. | " |
| CAPTAIN. | Mrs. Fennell, | Inniscarra, | CO. CORK. |

MEMBERS.

| | | |
|---|---|---|
| Mrs. Heagarty, | 7, Marguireta Villas, Dean Street, | Cork. |
| Miss M. Richardson, | Sullivan's Quay, | CORK. |
| " D. Manning, | Pouladuff Road, | " |
| " L. Murphy, | Do. | " |
| " S. O'Regan, | Togher, | " |
| " K. Donovan, | Togher? | " |
| Mrs. Forde, | 7, Barrack Street, | |
| Miss B. Collins, | U. S. A. | |
| Mrs. Kelleher, | Togher, | CORK. |
| Mrs. Tobin, | 79, Shandon Street, | " |

14

MEMBERSHIP ON 1ST JULY 1922.

| | |
|---|---|
| Mrs. Ahern, | 60, High Street, CORK. |
| Mrs. Tobin, | 79, Shandon Street, CORK. |

*We hereby certify that the above list is correct;*

*Mairgread Bean Uí Luasa. (Hon Sec Pensions Committee) 5 Sunray Ter. Blarney Street*
*(Mrs) Eileen Ahern (Late Treas of Lehenagh Branch) 60 High St.*
*(Mrs) Mary E. Hegarty (Late Pres. Cork Branch)*
*7 Minerva Ter. College Road.*

Cumann na mBan membership featuring Nan (Fennell) and Mamie (Forde)

CUMANN NA mBAN.

CORK DISTRICT COUNCIL.

MEMBERSHIP ON JULY 11TH 1921.

OFFICERS

| | | |
|---|---|---|
| PRESIDENT. | Mrs. Langford, Scotland. | TOMAS CEANNT BRANCH. |
| SECRETARY, | Miss M. Conlon 3459310466 Sunday's Well. | SHANDON BRANCH. |

MEMBERS.

| | | |
|---|---|---|
| Mrs. Martin, | Parnell Place, Cork. ) | CRAOBH POBLACHTAC |
| Miss E. Barry, | 5, Windsor Place, " ) | NA h-EIREANN. |
| Mrs. O'Mahoney, | Sheares Street, " ) | TOMAS MACCURTAIN |
| Miss N. Crowley. | 190, Blarney St., " ) | BRANCH. |
| Miss B. Richardson, | Sullivan's Quay, " ) | LEHENAGH BRANCH. |
| Mrs. Fennell, | Inniscarra, Co. Cork. ) | |
| Miss M. Aherne, | Highfield Ave., " ) | CORK BRANCH |
| " M. Bastible, | Dublin. ) | |
| Mrs. K. Deacy, | 8, Common's Road, Cork. | DUBLIN PIKE BRANCH. |
| Mrs. Linehan, | 50, Grand Parade, " | SHANDON BRANCH. |
| Mrs. McMahon, | Friar's Street, " | ST. FINBARR'S BRANCH. |
| Miss S. Kennedy, | | UNIVERSITY COLLEGE " |
| Miss E. O'Doherty, | 15, Shamrock Tce, Blarney, | BLARNEY BRANCH. |
| Mrs. O'Donovan, | Douglas West. | DOUGLAS BRANCH. |
| Mrs. Scott, (?) | Wellington Road, Cork. | ST. PATRICK'S BRANCH. |
| Mrs. Crowley, | Gurranabraher Road, " | BISHOPSTOWN'S " (WILTON) |
| Mrs. P. Sutton, | Loretto Ville, Glasheen Rd. | LOUGH BRANCH. [?] |
| ?- | - | BLACKROCK BRANCH. |

(Mrs.) Eileen Ahern (Late Treas Lehenagh Branch, 60, High St. Cork

(Mrs) Mary E. Hegarty) Late Pre. Cork Branch) 7 Minerva College Ter

Maugfread bean Uí Luasa (Hon Sec Pensions Committee)
5, Grery St. Blarney St. Cork

Cumann na mBan membership featuring Nan (Fennell) and Mamie (Forde)

# The Americans Arrive in Queenstown (Cobh)!

The sinking of the Lusitania off the Kinsale coast in May 1915 with the loss of American civilian lives helped to bring the United States of America into the First World War. In April 1917, they made a formal declaration of war against the German Empire. Queenstown (Cove) was the established naval base for the British, and, as a consequence, it also became the base for the American Navy; it established a naval destroyer division there. It and Castletownbere were already very important bases for the British Navy in their war effort.

There was, however, tension between both navies and their officers as the Americans came under British command. While their arrival created much-needed employment locally, they also created tension between themselves and the British servicemen. Being better paid, they were attracting a lot of social attention, not only from the locals but from observers as far away as Cork city.

With many Irish Americans amongst their ranks, they were also being accused officially, by local Sinn Féin activists, of while purporting to fight for the freedom of small nations were actually helping to suppress the cause of Irish independence. The Americans had entered the war on the principle that its outcome would ensure self-determination for all nations, great or small. Britain had made a similar pledge but as it transpired, not on their own doorstep.

The American Navy also used Queenstown as a stopover on their way back to the USA to bury their war casualties sustained in Europe. It was against this background that Mamie and her fiancé John Forde were able to silently, bravely, and without notice procure much-needed weapons and intelligence for 'H' Company and the Cork IRA Brigade.

Mamie was engaged to John Forde, a fellow Volunteer from 'H' Company, who at this time was employed by S. Monaghan, Midleton Street, Cove, General Funeral Establishment. This firm had the exclusive contract of embalming and supplying lead coffins to the Navy. John was responsible for all of the embalming, and he took this opportunity to source arms, ammunition and intelligence information from the many

Irish American sailors who expressed sympathy for the Irish cause. His privileged position provided him with opportunities to obtain valuable intelligence, which he and Mamie then passed on to the Brigade.

## GENERAL FUNERAL ESTABLISHMENT

MIDLETON STREET,
COVE (QUEENSTOWN). May 22"/1945

HABITS.
WREATHS
AND
CROSSES
SUPPLIED

MR, .........................................

To **S. MOYNIHAN**

Funeral Necessaries of the Late....................................

Dear Sir,
This is to certify that Mr John Forde now (Deceased) was in my employment for a number of years + full charge of my Undertaking establishment during the period of the Great War. when we handled all the Embalming of the American Sailors who lost their lives in our Harbour + around our Coast we Supplied them with Zad Lined + Lead Coffins, and this brought Mr Forde in close Contact with the Crews of the Ships in the Harbour who were in the position to give him the material he needed to help the old I.R.A, and I must say he availed of the opportunity...

Moynihan letters

It was not until 1919, when the Great War was over, that the last Americans who died and had been buried in Cove had their bodies exhumed and transferred back to the US. Mamie helped John to deliver the arms and ammunition to his workplace in Peter Street, Cork city, and subsequently carry them from there to her family ammunition dump at 'The Laurels' under John Joe's total control. Mamie often related to her son Denis (Dee) the story of when their own family undertaking business was established how the soldiers, after embalming, were dressed in military uniform, including side arms. Many of these arms never made it stateside, but instead found their way to 'The Laurels'.

After their marriage in June 1920, the couple continued to store arms but now also in their own new home in St Patrick's Terrace, Greenmount, which was not far from her parent's family home in Pouladuff. Their brave and dangerous actions provided the Cork Brigade with a constant supply of much-needed 'stuff' and valuable information over the years.

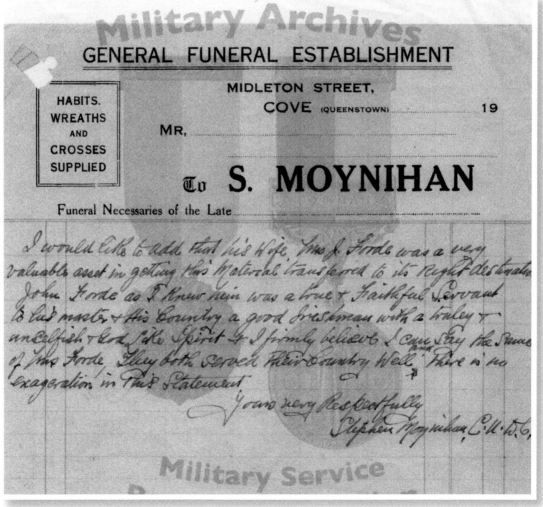

Moynihan letters

# Bomb and Landmine Factory

Throughout the war, 'The Laurels' was being used as a bomb-making factory, making mostly tin-can bombs and also as an ammunition and weapons dump. Many of the cans came from the Crosse & Blackwell factory, which was a well-known meat and fruit producer in Cork at that time. With the cooperation of their work colleagues, these cans were smuggled out of the factory by Cumann na mBan members who were working there. Landmines were also being manufactured on the premises.

# Cattle Raids

With 'The Laurels' now functioning as an established intelligence hub, there developed an increased local resistance in the area to the British Army, especially when they attempted to raid farms in order to export cattle to England. One such recorded incident happened on the Pouladuff Road, when the Hussy farm, close neighbours of the Hegartys, was the victim of an attempted raid. John Joe, along with Joe Murphy and other members of 'H' Company, led an armed party of volunteers against the army to prevent the theft of their cattle. These determined men took up their armed positions at the entrance to the fields and threatened all to enter at their peril. Through the use of similar intelligence work and tactics, the company prevented further cattle raids on the farms of the Magners and, more dangerously, the Hosfords, whose farm was adjacent to the local RIC barracks on the Togher Road.

These decisive actions resulted in the cessation of cattle raids in their area - these operations were all carried out under The Export Prevention Order. Pouladuff and surrounding areas would soon be effectively under the control of the IRA.

John Joe's sections were also under orders to disrupt the delivery of cattle going to Ballincollig Barracks as the Brigade had put a levy of £150 on all seizures.

RAIDS FOR CATTLE - (Export Prevention Order) Hussey's, Magner's and Hosford's.

| | |
|---|---|
| Jos. Richardson. | Co. Waterford. |
| Jerome Hurley. | |
| Edward Barrett. | Lehanagh. |
| Jerh. Callanan. | ¬t. Merrion, Dublin. |
| Tim Hurley. | Mallow. |
| Con Murphy. | |
| Denis Callanan. | Lough Rd. |
| Jas. Hennessy. | George's Quay. |
| Chris. Hennessy. | Pouladuff. |
| John J. Hegarty. | do. |
| Thomas Murphy. | do. |
| Thomas Collins. | |
| Dan Coveney. | Lehenagh. |
| Tim Ahern. | do. |
| Thomas Leahy. | Greenmount. |
| Con O'Regan. | |

Cattle Raids

H. Coy. 2nd. Batt.

Seizure of Cattle (Brigade Levy of £150.)

| | |
|---|---|
| Edward Barrett. | Lehenagh. |
| Jerh. Callanan. | Mt. Merrion Park, Dublin. |
| Chris. Hennessxy. | Pouladuff. |
| John J. Hegarty. | do. |
| Con O'Callaghan. | U.S.A. |
| Tom Murphy. | Pouladuff. |

# Section Commander

During 1918, John Joe was appointed a Section Commander and Lieutenant of 'H' Company 2nd Battalion 1st Cork Brigade at the age of 21, where he had sixty men under his command. He continued making bombs and landmines, storing arms, and also forging croppy pikes at 'The Laurels'.

These works were well within his competence as a blacksmith, which was a required skill for all market gardeners, especially those who owned horses. These pikes were made famous during the rebellion of 1798. While being no substitute for guns, which were in short supply at that time, they were nevertheless formidable and dangerous weapons.

| Thomas Leahy | 2nd Lieut. |
| Con. O'Callaghan | Sect. Commdr. (No. 1 Section) |
| John J. Hegarty | do. (No. 2 Section) |
| Tim. Hurley | do. (No. 3 Section) |
| Jerh. Callanan | do. (No. 4 Section) -formerly acted as 1st Lieutenant. |
| Co. Quartermaster | Tim. Hobbs.(lieu Jerh. Long) |
| Co. Adjutant | Owen Callanan. |

*cntr at) date
d do .*

9

## No. One Section.

/Edward Barrett (above) BALLYPEHANE
/Thos. Murphy POULADUFF, RD, CORK.
2/Jerh. Murphy POULADUFF, RD, CORK
/C. Hennessy POULADUFF, RD, CORK
2/Tim. Ahern LEHENAGH, CORK,
/J. Donovan LEHENAGH, CORK,
/J. Moran FAIRYVILLE LOUGH RD CORK
2/Walsh LEHENAGHMORE Co CORK
/A. Walsh LEHENAGHMORE Co CORK
/D. Jackson ELFORD, DAGENHAM, ESSEX, Eng
/Lar. Hurley ASHGROVE Co CORK
/John Hurley CAPWELL RD CORK
/Patk. Hurley OLIVERPLUNKET ST CORK
/Patk. Healy U.S.A
/M. Lonergan DOUGLAS Co CORK
/D. Lonergan DOUGLAS Co CORK
/J. Ryan QUARRY LANE CORK
/David Sheehan POULADUFF, RD, CORK
2/Con. O'Callaghan (above) U.S.A
2/Jerh. O'Connor TOGHER, RD, CORK
/Dan. Mullane
/Jerh. Mullane LEHENAGH Co CORK
/Jos. O'Callaghan LEHENAGH Co CORK
/Dan. Coveney BLARNEY Co CORK
/Willie Harvey THE COTTAGE, GLASHEEN, RD
/Son. Manning R.I.P
/J. Brady TOGHER RD CORK
/Chas. Feeney HIBERNIAN BLDGS CORK

26

/Maurice Sexton, DOUGHCLOYNE, Co
/John Collins c/o QUEENS OLD CAST
/Tim. Donovan USA
/Harry Lane, TOGHER, CROSS, Co
/Harry Harvey TOGHER, RD, CORK
1/2 J. Buckley U.S.A
/J. Sullivan U.S.A
/P. Sexton TOGHER, RD CORK
/M. Buckley TOGHER, RD CORK
/Jerh. Crowley
X /Willl Regan TOGHER, RD, CORK
/Ml. Cronin TOGHER, RD, CORK
/Jerh. J. Murphy KINSALE ROCK
/M. Coveney KNOCKLASHEEN CORK
/D. O'Leary TOGHER, RD, CORK
/J. Coveney R.I.P
/D. O'Sullivan U.S.A
1/2 Dan. Feeney TOGHER, RD, COR
/John Crowley TOGHER RD CORK
/D. Murphy TOGHER RD CORK
/Thos. Collins HOLLYVILLE CURRA
1/2 Chas. Harvey U.S.A
1/2 Con. Regan 33, DUBLIN ST CORK
/Sean Scanlon
/Son. Leahy R.I.P
/Tim. O'Connor R.I.P
/Jim Neill LEHENAGH CORK

27

## No. Two Section.

Daniel Murphy (above) G.S.RLY ATHLONE
John J. Hegarty (above) POULADUFF, RD,
Jas. Hennessy GEORGES QUAY CORK

John Kelleher POULADUFF RD CORK
Michael Lyons R.I.P
John Murphy LEHENAGHBEG Co CORK

H Company Record

# Intelligence Work

At about this time, John Joe was appointed Intelligence Officer in 'H' Company, and as both his sisters were by now also intelligence officers in Cumann na mBan, 'The Laurels' became a vital cog in the Brigade's overall intelligence network.

As a market gardener, John Joe was making deliveries of vegetables and fresh goods to city markets and also, more importantly, to the local RIC Barracks. His regular and familiar movements around the city using his horse and cart for transport would not have aroused enemy suspicion. He had access to places occupied by the enemy forces and their agents and was picking up useful information, which he passed on to the Brigade commanders, which at that time was led by Tomas Mac Curtain. Nan and Mamie were also busy building up their further networks, not only in Cork but in Tipperary and other counties.

In all conflicts, intelligence work is vital, and those at the coalface of such activity are often overlooked when history is written or discussed. During the War Of Independence against the might of the British Empire, it was certainly a very dangerous role, with their lives constantly being placed at risk. Not only were they providing information on British troops and RIC activity, but they also identified British spies and suspected informers who would later be possibly eliminated.

The intimidation of people was also now an important role, as passing on information to the British authorities or their agents was as good as a death sentence. This helped to reinforce the idea that the RIC, and by extension the British State, could no longer protect certain sections of Irish society.

The IRA had instigated a guerrilla war against the British Empire and, as a consequence, did not or could not hold prisoners for any undue length of time. Therefore life and death decisions had to be made in all doubtful cases with no middle ground between release or execution. Reliable intelligence work was vital and one of the reasons for bringing the War of Independence to an end.

The importance of intelligence gathering is also further endorsed by Lawrence James in his *The Rise and Fall of the British Empire*[2]. In it he analyses the reasons the British agreed to the Truce: 'The British army had still not overcome many of its operational problems, not least the lack of a competent intelligence-gathering service. In fact, by early June, the two sides were facing deadlock.'

This was further endorsed by the anti-Treaty Todd Andrews, when he declared, 'For the first time in the history of separatism, we Irish had a better intelligence service than the British. This was Michael Collins' great achievement, and it is one for which every Irishman should honour his memory.'

It can never be underestimated how important the intelligence-gathering network established nationwide by Michael Collins was in securing independence. In Dublin, for example, he would meet some of his intelligence officers in a Church of Ireland maternity hospital. Who would ever suspect single men with flowers visiting such a hospital?

The State became almost paralysed and unable to function effectively as a result of the Irish intelligence network established under Collins. The Hegarty siblings and their parents all played their part in this intelligence network. They gathered information in the city and carried dispatches to and from the different Cork Brigade officers to James Leahy of the Tipperary Brigade. 'The Laurels' was, in fact, an intelligence hub for information, with letters being sent to Nan from Leahy for ongoing delivery to the Brigade.

It was during 1966, the fiftieth anniversary of the Easter Rising, that I asked John Joe what his views were of Michael Collins, knowing he had taken the anti-Treaty side. We had just returned from Collins Barracks after the ceremonies to mark the Rising's golden jubilee. The Barracks was the centre point of Cork celebrations, with an Old IRA officer and the then Minister for External Affairs Frank Aiken taking the parade salute. He told me he had huge respect for him, as we all should, and to always remember his bravery. He did add, however, 'He is one of Ireland's greatest soldiers to be admired by all and was a master of intelligence gathering. But as a politician, I did not agree with his views.'

2    ISBN 9780351314292

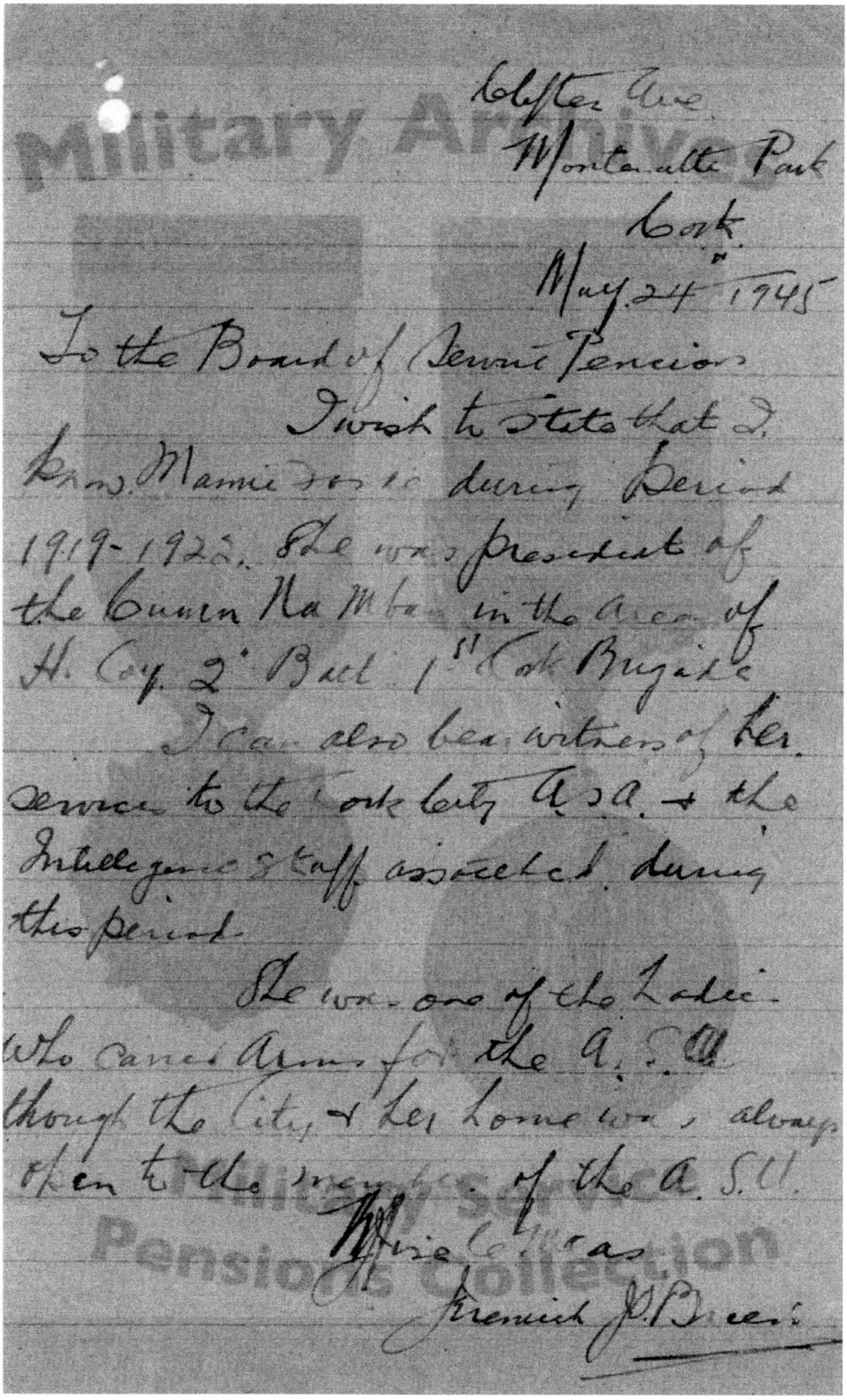

Clifton Ave.
Montenotte Park
Cork.
May 24th 1945

To the Board of Service Pension

I wish to state that I know Mamie ___ during Period 1919-1922. She was president of the Cumann Na M ba in the area of H. Coy 2nd Batt 1st Cork Brigade

I can also bear witness of her service to the Cork City A.S.U. + the Intelligence Staff associated during this period

She was one of the Ladies who carried Arms for the A.S.U though the City + her home was always open to the members of the A.S.U.

Mise le meas

Jeremiah J. Brien

Jerry O'Brien's Letter

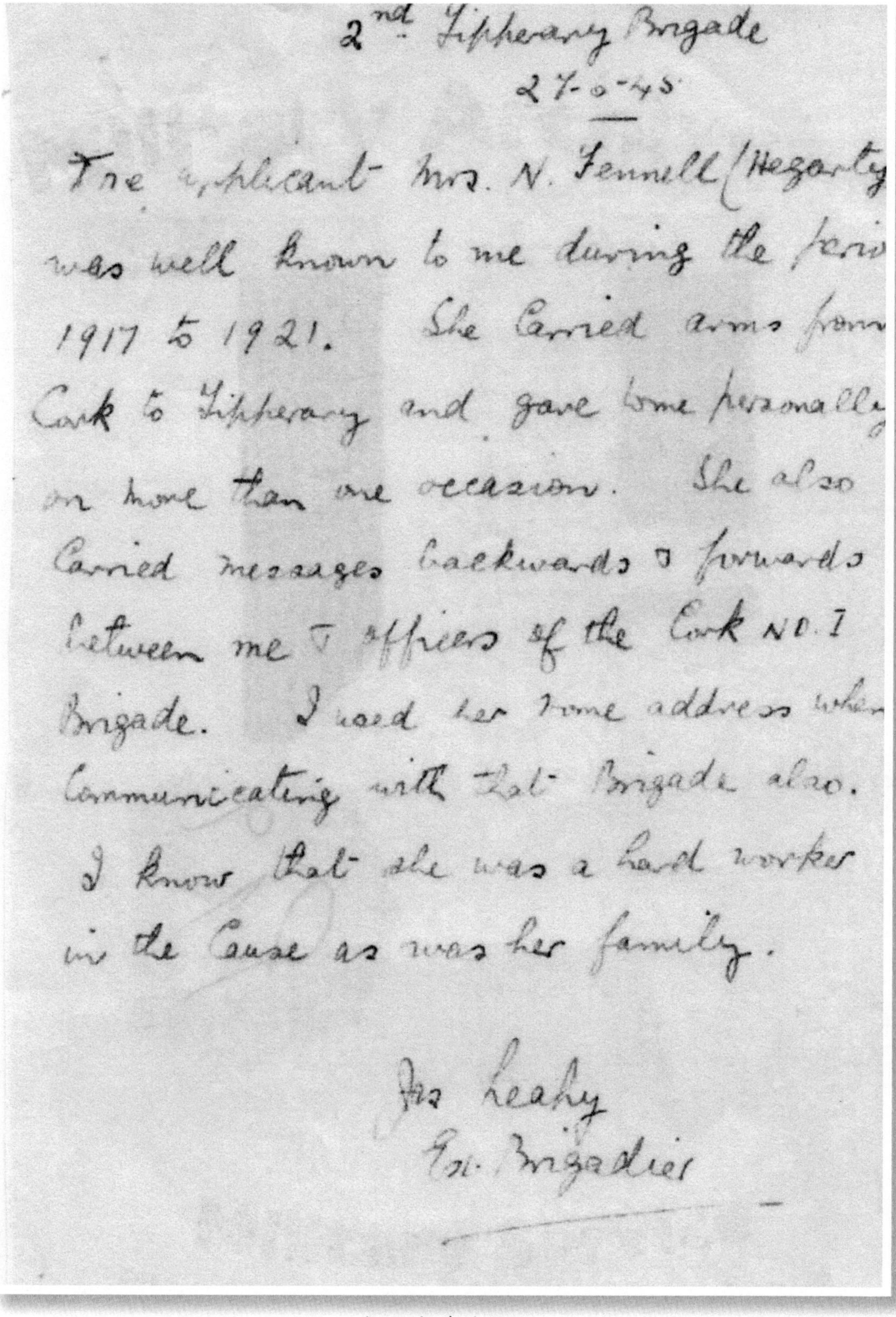

2nd Tipperary Brigade
27-5-45

The applicant Mrs. N. Fennell (Hegarty) was well known to me during the period 1917 to 1921. She carried arms from Cork to Tipperary and gave some personally on more than one occasion. She also carried messages backwards & forwards between me & officers of the Cork No. 1 Brigade. I used her home address when communicating with 1st Brigade also. I know that she was a hard worker in the Cause as was her family.

Jas Leahy
Ex Brigadier

James Leahy Letter

Cof.g.

Kerry Pike,
Carrigrohan, Cork.
26 - 6 - 45.

To Whom it may Concern.

I wish to state that Mr Nan Fennell née Hegarty gave excellent help to the I.R.A. during the tan + Civil war period. On various occasions taking guns + ammo. from my house then (Clark: Bdge address) where I held a very big dump for my own Company + also for Bttl., to outskirts of City often for immidiate use., + collecting same + talking home to temporary dump.

On one occassion in winter of 1920 we attacked Elizabeth Fort Bks. I afterward handed over four revolvers to Nan Hegarthy at Greenmount school by arrangement + skipped home myself knowing guns were quite safe.

This help was inestimable to me during 1920 + 1921. as there were a number of spies in area who were properly dealt with. in consequence there were a few men on the run who were taken by Nan Hegarthy to her Aunt house in Killingly.

During Civil war Mrs Mitchell + she took Ammo to me while operating in the third Bdg. area

I cannot at this stage detail all the work done by Nan Hegarthy. when we were badly in need of such help. Neither can I speak too highly of the efficient way in which many little problems were got over by her + her sister, men on the run were looked after. stuff dropped into house + had to be put away quickly + soon. + the all important feature there was never a slip. The home was much used being in the suburbs of City.

Signed      Herbert J. Mitchell
             Sen.

Sean Mitchell Letter

~ 42 ~

Kerry Pike
Carrigrohane.
Cork
31/5/45

To Whome it may Concern.

I wish to state thate to my
knowledge. Mrs Mary Forde did much usiful
work for the I.R.A at a time when we were
in need of such help.

On several occassions she
brought parcels of ammunition & on one occassi
Revalouvrs from Coabh to her husbands store
in Peter St Cork, This stuff was given to
her by her husband who was then working
in Cobh.

I was in close tuch witch her fami
as house was much used as a call house. Being
in the Suburbs & on the way to Country

Signe Herbert Mitchell
Comdt,

Sean (Herbert) Mitchell Letter

~ 43 ~

# Raids for Active Service Units

John Joe and 'H' Company were involved in many raids for arms, motorcars, and bicycles on various occasions in homes and commercial premises in Cork, such as Hosford, Hayes, Coughlan, Morrisson, White, Ronayne, Browne, O'Brien, Tate, Daly, Marshes, O'Hea's Garage, and Cork Grammar School on the Wellington Road.

The result of which saw many of the guns and ammunition finding their way to 'The Laurels'. This enabled the section under his command to have proper rifle practice. Having secured sufficient arms for his own section, the remainder were supplied to 1st Brigade Flying Columns, their Active Service Unit (ASU), of which he was also an active member when his intelligence activities in the city allowed.

## H. Coy. 2nd. Batt.

Raids for Arms, Motor Cars and Cycles on various occasions.

(Hosford, Hayes, Coughlan, Morrisson, White, Ronayne, Browne, O'Brien, Tate, Daly, Marshes, O'Hea's Garage, etc.)

| | |
|---|---|
| Edward Barrett. | Lehanagh. |
| Dan Murphy. | Athlone. |
| Jerh. Calanan. | Mt. Merrion Park, Dublin. |
| John J. Hegarty. | Pouladuff Rd. |
| Denis Callanan. | 45, Lough Rd. |
| Patrick O'Connell. | The Lough. |
| Thomas Leahy. | Greenmount. |
| Thomas Collins. | |
| Timy. Hurley. | Sugar Beet Factory, Mallow. |
| Michael Buckley. | Athlone. |
| Chris. Hennessy. | Pouladuff Rd. |
| Jas. Hennessy. | George's Quay. |
| Jerh. O'Brien. | Clifden Rd. |
| Tim Ahern. | Lehanagh. |
| Dan Coveney. | do. |
| Jerh. Connors. | do. |
| Con O'Regan. | Blackpool. |
| Con O'Callaghan. | U.S.A. |

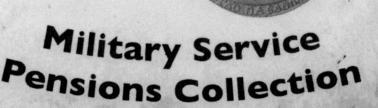

H. Coy. 2nd. Batt.

Raid at Gipsy Camp, Glasheen.

| | |
|---|---|
| Jos. Richardson. | Co. Waterford. |
| Jerome Hurley. | |
| Con Murphy. | |
| Jerh. Callanan. | Mount Merrion Park, Dublin. |
| Edward Barrett. | Lehenagh. |
| Tim Hurley. | Mallow. |
| John J. Hegarty. | Pouladuff. |
| Denis Callanan. | Lough Rd. |
| Jerh. O'Brien. | Clifden Avenue. |
| Chris. Hennessy. | Pouladuff. |
| Jas. Hennessy. | George's Quay. |
| Michael Buckley. | Athlone. |
| Tim Ahern. | Lehanagh. |
| Dan Coveney. | do. |
| Con O'Regan. | |

(& probably 20 others.)

# Murray's Gun Shop Raid

One of the Volunteers' more audacious raids, where 'H' Company played its part, was at the premises of T.W. Murray, Gunsmiths, 87 Patrick Street, which took place on the evening of 18th November 1919. A number of Volunteer units were involved in the raid and managed to get away with a large number of guns and ammunition. The shop was situated only a few minutes away from the RIC Barracks on Tuckey Street, but even so, it was sometime before the raid was reported.

Sean O'Sullivan, a volunteer with 'B' Company, played a vital role in this operation. (Incidentally, years later, John Joe's son Eddie married Sean's daughter Mary.) To commemorate the raid one hundred years later to the day, the grandson of both men, John Joseph Hegarty, revisited the shop.

Another of 'H' and 'G' Company raids for arms was recorded at the Gipsy Camp on the Magazine Road in Glasheen as they understood there were a number of shotguns on-site to be secured.

John Joseph Hegarty outside Murrays on the centenary of the raid

# A Brigade Meeting House

'The Laurels' was now also becoming a meeting place for brigade officers, including men such as Sean O'Hegarty, Tom Crofts, Con Neenan, and Sean Mitchell, and officers from other brigades outside the county, such as the Tipperary officers James Leahy, Jack Meagher, and M. Molloy.

Meagher had been arrested defending his commanding officer James Leahy (later to become his brother-in-law, after James married his sister Josephine), who had called to his home in Annefield when it was raided by the RIC. As a result, he was sentenced to six months in Cork jail.

Jerry O'Brien, another intelligence officer in 'H' Company, recorded that he stayed there once a week and that it was being used by others on a regular basis. It was ordered, therefore, that the house now needed to be heavily guarded by volunteers to protect those attending these meetings. Sean O'Hegarty, Commanding Officer of the Brigade after the death of the much-admired Terence MacSwiney, remembers using it as his office during the daytime, with Nan available for any dispatches required, and then returning to the city HQ during the evening and night time.

# Gardens & Sheds Readied for War

On the few rare occasions that he spoke about the 'troubles,' John Joe pointed out to family members places of concealment in the market gardens. He told us that one of the vegetables that were specifically planted was celery; as he explained, this allowed Volunteers or men 'on the run' to lie between the deep drills to hide whenever a raid occurred.

This is a practice he continued for the rest of his life and the reason why our celery stalks were always white, having been earthed so high. Trenches were also dug along all hedgerows, especially those bordering our sympathetic neighbours and friends the Russell family. They were always no higher than waist height to allow for easy access and escape. These and the hen run allowed further options of cover. A bunker was also built under the potato and mangold pits to hide both arms and men. He explained that when the Tans or army prodded their bayonets into them, they only hit what was above ground. He also said they hid arms in the piggery, a very successful ploy as the raiders were never anxious to thoroughly search it for obvious reasons!

Juleann (Russell) Cunningham. Her brothers Jack and Sonny Russell were also members of Company H

# Nan Goes Full -Time with Cumann na mBan

By this stage, all the Hegarty siblings had experience as intelligence operatives and had a growing reputation for helping the Active Service Units (ASU), providing invaluable information on enemy troops and their spy agents locally, and securing a continuous supply of arms and ammunition.

Nan, by now, had given up her career ambitions and devoted herself full-time to the cause, investing all her time and energies into the work of Cumann na mBan, with her parents Patrick and Elizabeth supporting her financially during this period.

She had by now also progressed to carrying parcels of arms, ammunition and grenades, and intelligence-briefs dispatches between the Cork, Tipperary, and Limerick brigades.

The Referee.

Application Of Mrs M F Forde Kaiser's Hill
Barrack St — Cork

I am aware that Mrs Ford (nee Hegarty) was
a very active member Of the Cumann
na mBan in Cork City.
During the years Of 1917 and 1918 she
was very active in organising functions to
raise funds for The volunteers. Her house
in Pouladuff (outskirts Of the City) was very
extensively used for communication with
the 9th Batt area Herself and sister handled
very many despatches. Her house was very
constantly used by the Brigade O/c Sean
Hegarty in company with other Officers.
In 1920 she was a constant visitor
with comforts to I R A prisoners and also
housed men on the run including Meagher
Molloy and others from Tipperary & Limerick
&c. She carried ammunition on several
occasions from her husbands stores who
procured it from U.S. Soldiers Sailors
at Cobh. She was constantly bringing this
ammunition from Cobh to Cork. (Her husband
was working at Cobh)
She procured a Rifle the property
of an ex British Soldier in Blarney
She discovered it in his house and had
it removed to Cork City.

~ 51 ~

Towards the end of the Tan period she married and then resided in Emeacumnt also in The suburbs. She continued to keep I R A light and day and continued to carry ammunition.

I have no hesitation in saying That Mrs Fords claim is an outstanding one and I would be very pleased to give evidence on her behalf.

Tom Crofts.

# The Tipperary Brigade Connections

Commandant James Leahy No 2 (Mid) Tipperary Brigade reported that he corresponded with Nan at 'The Laurels' in order to pass messages to the Cork Brigade commanders who were using 'The Laurels' as their meeting house. He believed that she and the family were hard workers for the cause and completely trustworthy.

Leahy led a very active volunteer unit in Tipperary and he was arrested and jailed on a number of occasions. He spent time on hunger strike in Belfast jail with Thomas Ashe. On his release, James did not leave the jail empty-handed as he stole the spoon they were trying

Commandant James Leahy

to feed him with - it's still in the family's possession. The only spoons issued were wooden. Ordinary knives and spoons were not issued presumably in case prisoners used them as weapons against their guards or had suicidal tendencies. As well as eating with the spoons, some prisoners used them to bore holes in cell walls.

On their release from prison, It was not unusual for republican prisoners to attempt to steal keepsakes of their time in jail.

In his book *Allegiance*, Robert Brennan gives an account of taking a prayer book and of JJ Walsh leaving the prison wearing his civilian clothes over his convicts uniform.

On another occasion, on the 4th March 1918, James escaped from Crown forces in Thurles by leaping into the river Suir, and swimming to the other side with the

James Stapleton

enemy in hot pursuit. In 1991 an event was organised by 'The Spirit of Tipperary Society' to commemorate, and a plaque was unveiled by Cathal MacSwiney Brugha.

On one particular occasion, under instructions from another Tipperary officer, Capt. John Meagher, who also confirms staying at 'The Laurels', Nan was ordered to hand a parcel of ammunition to Vice Commandant James Stapleton of No 2 Brigade, Tipperary. James (Jimmy) Stapleton, a man described by Leahy as always anxious for a fight, was responsible for the execution of two notable Tipperary RIC district inspectors, namely Wilson and Hunt.

As a result of Hunt's shooting on 23rd June 1919, the government proclaimed martial law in the Thurles district, with immediate reinforcements being dispatched to the area.

The Tipperary IRA Brigades' campaigns benefited from Nan's bravery and commitment when she risked her own life bringing dispatches, weapons and ammunition from the arms dump at 'The Laurels'.

Nan always took the train when travelling from Cork to Tipperary, using the Sarsfield family as cover for her operations. She was also in contact with Dan Breen, another of the leading Tipperary officers. Breen took part in the Soloheadbeg Ambush, where the first deaths in the War of Independence were recorded. He once had a price of £10,000 on his head. The same man took a very active anti-Treaty position during the Civil War and issued an appeal to his former comrades in the Free State Army. He later became a Fianna Fáil TD.

These men were some of the leading volunteers in Tipperary during the War of Independence and the Civil War. Leahy's son Seamus, a former teacher in Rockwell College, told me the reason his father chose the anti-Treaty side in the Civil War was because of the bombing of the Four Courts in Dublin. He said his parents were returning home from their honeymoon in Killarney via Cork at the time of the Truce in order to visit James's brother Mick and others, including Sean Hegarty, OC of the Cork Brigade, to discuss the different, difficult options and decisions confronting all volunteers.

Then the news came of Collins' orders to bomb the Four Courts in Dublin. James immediately cut short his honeymoon and decided to return home to organise the anti-Treaty IRA in Tipperary. A number of James' comrades, men such as Michael Joseph Costelloe, a Tipperary intelligence officer, took the Treaty side.

Mick Leahy had moved to Cork in 1919 and was the manager of Wren's Hotel on Winthrop Street. Coming from a family steeped in nationalism and the GAA, he soon joined the Cork Brigade of the IRA and became an intelligence officer, similar to the Hegarty siblings. When the hotel was raided on the night of the 11th and the 12th of December 1920, the night Cork was burned, a knock came to the door of the hotel. When Mick answered and gave his name, he was shot at. He escaped being murdered but was shot in the arm by a drunken Black and Tan. It's worth noting that Mick was an accomplished hurler who went on to play with Blackrock Hurling Club and had the distinction of representing his native county Tipperary and Cork at senior level. His son, also Mick, years later was the owner of the Courthouse Tavern Bar and played with St. Finbarr's, Gaelic Athletic Association (GAA) Club.

It should be remembered that the GAA, despite being a non-political organisation as it is today, was instrumental in promoting nationalism and, indeed, some would say independence as it allowed men to gather in public to play and support the playing of games for both parish and county. The volunteers had to use hurleys instead of rifles for drill practice as arms were in short supply.

The most noteworthy involvement of the Association was on 21st November 1920 at its headquarters in Croke Park, when a match between Dublin and Tipperary was arranged for that Sunday afternoon. That morning, however, the IRA under the command of Michael Collins organised an operation to eliminate a group of undercover British intelligence agents known as the 'Cairo Gang'.

The operation was successful, in so far as up to fifteen agents were killed or fatally wounded. Many more, in a state of panic, fled to the safety of Dublin Castle.

Linking the IRA to the GAA, the authorities ordered a raid on the spectators in Croke Park. Without warning, the forces opened fire on both attendees and players, killing fourteen and wounding sixty to seventy others, including women and children. Despite the fact that all witnesses claimed the forces opened fire without provocation, the British authorities accepted the police report that they had been fired on first. The massacre on that afternoon is now referred to in Irish history as Bloody Sunday and was responsible for increasing more popular support for the IRA and the desire for independence.

Many of today's GAA grounds have been named to celebrate those who fought for Irish freedom and national sovereignty, such as the Barr's Neenan Park, and nationwide; Pearse Stadium, Markievicz Park, and McHale Park. In Cork, similar to other counties, there are a number of clubs, such as Fr. O'Callaghan's and Delaney's, named after the dead patriots. Cork city board also runs the MacSwiney and Mac Curtain cups competitions each year to commemorate the two patriots. Thus maintaining and celebrating the strong links. When the GAA club Glen Rovers was founded in 1916, they added a black band to their jersey in tribute to those who had died during the rising of the same year. It is a tradition that continues to this day.

After the Civil War, the Association helped reconcile both factions at both club and inter-county levels.

The morning operation inflicted severe damage on the British intelligence network, not only in Dublin but nationwide. Collins, when asked about the operation at a later stage, declared, 'There is no crime in detecting and destroying in wartime the spy and informer. They have destroyed without trial. I have paid them back in their own coin.'

Cathal MacSwiney Brugha unveiling Leahy plaque in Thurles 1991

***Prison Spoon***

A spoon issued to Irish Volunteer James Leahy when he was interred in Belfast Jail in 1918. He is later quoted as follows: "This spoon was issued to me with an enamel mug and plate when I was booked into the jail and it was the only property I was able to get away with on my release. Ordinary knives and spoons were not issued, presumably in case prisoners had suicidal tendencies. As well as eating with it, prisoners used it to bore holes in cell walls."

Loaned by Seamus Leahy

L.387.1

Leahy's spoon

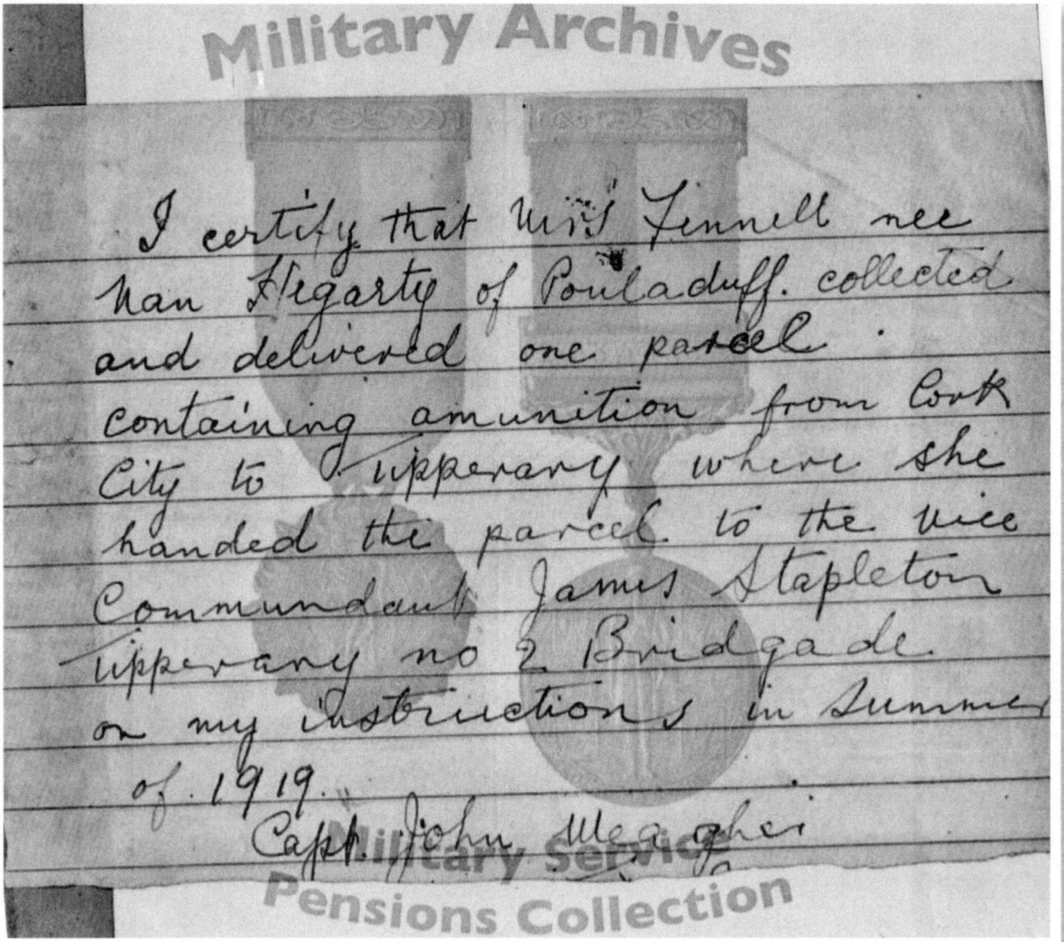

I certify that Mrs Finnell nee Nan Hegarty of Pouladuff. collected and delivered one parcel. containing amunition from Cork City to Tipperary where she handed the parcel. to the Vice Commundant James Stapleton Tipperary no 2 Bridgade. on my instructions in Summer of 1919.

Capt John Meagher

Jack Meagher's letter

Michael Leahy, Tubberadora, Boherlahan. He joined the Thurles Volunteers and then became a member of the Cork No. 1 Brigade, and was shot by Black and Tans in the hotel where he was manager on June 25th. 1921, but recovered sufficiently to resume activities as a Volunteer.

Michael Leahy

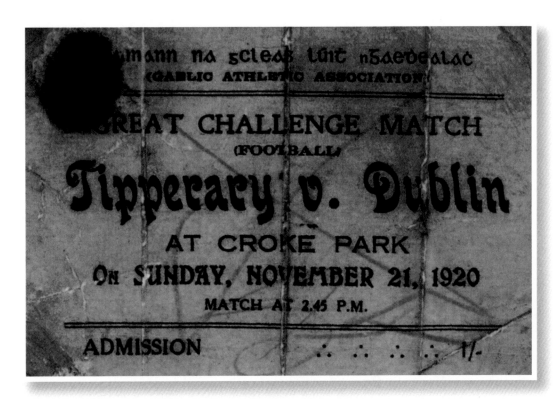

Match Ticket

# Sarsfield Family

Nan often accompanied members of Captain Sarsfield's family when she was travelling by train from Togher to Dublin for military manoeuvres. The Sarsfields were sympathetic to the cause. As a leading Cork landowning Church of Ireland family and children of a military officer with refined English accents, they were ideal travelling companions as they provided excellent cover. Their carriage was never searched when the trains were frequently stopped by either the British Army or the Black and Tans.

This gave Nan freedom of movement without drawing attention to herself and her parcels of arms on her dangerous journeys. John Joe often mentioned the special relationship Nan had with the Sarsfield family; not only were they travelling companions, but they also facilitated her by allowing her to store arms and ammunition on their property in Togher.

The British neither suspected nor questioned them as they simply saw their place as a hive of activity where local labourers worked and occasionally met socially. Consequently, their home was never raided or burned by either the IRA, the Black and Tans, or the British Army, all for totally different reasons.

The family also supported the Cork National Hunt Club, which comprised many local volunteers and supporters, including John Joe and his father among its members. Not only did they provide financial assistance to the club, but they also allowed them to use their lands for draghunts, and they provided kennels on their estate for some members' dogs.

On the 12th of December 1929, a few years after the formation of the Free State, The Pouladuff Coursing Club was established. Later it was renamed The Pouladuff and Bishopstown Coursing Club. The Sarsfields, in line with neighbouring farmers, continued to support their local community by leasing their lands for coursing and game preserves exclusively for the benefit of the club. They also continued their support of the community by allowing school children to use the field adjacent to the national school as a playground.

During my time at the school during the late fifties and early sixties, we used it as our football pitch at breaktime and after school, but we were always mindful of the cow dung! This field was never cultivated as a very generous gesture to the school. When trees were felled on their property, it was not unusual for permission to be given to locals to remove the timber for their own use.

Minutes Coursing Club meeting 1929

A meeting was held on Dec 12th 1929 for the purpose of establishing a coursing club and appointed the following officers and committee

| | |
|---|---|
| President | Mr. A. Russell |
| Chairman | Mr. D. J. O'Connell |
| Hon-Trea | E. Russell |
| Hon-Sec | E. Tyne |

Committee

Messrs.
R. Russell. John Fitzgerald. Jim Carroll. Tom Fitzgerald. J. O'Sullivan. Jerry Fitzgerald. John Foley. Ted O'Connell,

Slippers
Ted O'Connell. Jerry Fitzgerald.

Meets

| Grange Cross | Dec 15th 1929 | — 8 hare. |
|---|---|---|
| Corcoran Bridge | " 22nd " | — 5 " |
| Rathnacullig | " 29st " | — 4 " |
| Chetwynd | Jan 5st 1930 | — 5 " |
| Ballinvuskig cross | " 12 " | no meet |
| " " | " 19th " | — 1 har |
| Flower Garden | " 26st " | — 5 har |
| Douglas School | Febr 6st | — 6 " |
| Dougheloyne | " 9st " | — 6 " |
| Farmers Cross | " 16st " | — 5 " |
| Ballinvuskig cross | " 23st " | — 2 " |
| Close season. | | Total 47 |

Meets 10,
Arthur Russell
25/9/30

~ 62 ~

# 1920 - The Year Cork Went from Relative Peace to Guerrilla Warfare

Tomás Mac Curtain

In the local elections held in January 1920, Sinn Féin won 30 of the total 56 seats on the Cork Corporation, and then on the 30th of January, Tomás Mac Curtain was elected the first republican Lord Mayor of Cork. His first proposal in office at the City Hall was to recognise Dáil Eireann as the legal, constitutional parliament of the Irish Nation. This set the tone for significant future events that occurred later in the city. All the Hegarty family, together with all of 'H' Company and the Brigade, were very proactive in these elections.

Within a very few short weeks of his election on the 20th of March 1920, incidentally, his 36th birthday, the Lord Mayor Tomás Mac Curtain was murdered at his home in Blackpool in front of his pregnant wife and family by members of the RIC.

One of the volunteers sent later that evening to protect Mac Curtain's family was Sean O'Sullivan. O'Sullivan, a volunteer in 'B' Company, formed the guard of honour at the City Hall. The 'B' Company's role at the funeral was to act as bodyguards while Nan, in full uniform, also played her part by marching in military formation.

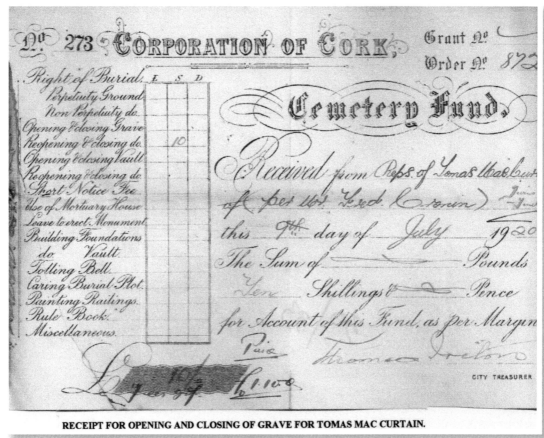

**RECEIPT FOR OPENING AND CLOSING OF GRAVE FOR TOMAS MAC CURTAIN.**

Tomás Mac Curtain Funeral receipt of Tomás Mac Curtain. Part of Hegarty Collection

# A Republican Plot in St Finbarr's Cemetery

On the day after the murder of Lord Mayor Tomas Mac Curtain in March 1920, the Brigade officers and, in particular, Fred Cronin (undertaker) requested that Cork Corporation donate and make available a plot as the burial place for the dead patriot. This was immediately agreed upon, and the site at St Finbarr's Cemetery was made available. Sean Mitchell was chief marshal at the cemetery plot. Seats had been prearranged for the Mac Curtain family. However, as the funeral cortege advanced very slowly, Mrs. Mac Curtain asked Sean to allow the guard of honour to walk around a little as it was very cold, an extraordinary altruistic gesture considering she and her young family were saying a final goodbye to their loved one. Mac Curtain would not be the last volunteer or indeed lord mayor to be buried there before the year was over. This plot is now known as the republican plot at St. Finbarr's Cemetery in Glasheen.

Sean O' Sullivan (pictured bottom right) Guard of Honour.  Credit Cork Examiner.

# Inquest & The Pursuit of Swanzy

When the inquest took place, it became apparent very quickly that the local RIC, and, in particular, Detective Inspector Oswald Swanzy, were responsible for Mac Curtain's murder. On the 17th of April, James J. McCabe read out the following verdict:

'We find that the late Alderman Tomás Mac Curtain, Lord Mayor of Cork, died from shock and haemorrhage, caused by bullet wounds, and that he was wilfully murdered under circumstances of the most callous brutality, and that the murder was organised and carried out by the Royal Irish Constabulary, officially directed by the British government, and we return a verdict of wilful murder against David Lloyd George, Prime Minister of England; Lord French, Lord Lieutenant of Ireland; Ian McPherson, late Chief Secretary of Ireland Acting Inspector - General Smith of the Royal Irish Constabulary, Divisional Inspector Clayton of the Royal Irish Constabulary, District Inspector Swanzy, and some unknown members of the Royal Irish Constabulary. We strongly condemn the system at present in vogue of carrying out raids at unreasonable hours. We tender to Mrs. Mac Curtain and family our sincerest sympathy in their terrible bereavement; this sympathy we extend to the citizens of Cork in the loss they have sustained by the death of one so eminently capable of directing their civil administration.'

As it was an informal inquest, no one was ever charged, but it is recorded that Swanzy was transferred from Cork under an assumed name. It was again the Cork Brigades' intelligence unit that discovered he was resident in Lisburn, a strong Unionist town just outside Belfast. The IRA were not prepared to let matters rest.

Michael Collins ordered Swanzy's assassination and volunteers from Cork took up the order. One of them was Sean Culhane. Culhane was the B Company's intelligence officer. He was already responsible for discovering Swanzy's new residence, and he was also the man who was, through his intelligence network, responsible for the execution of the notorious RIC Divisional Commissioner Smyth. With Culhane in charge, a unit travelled first to Dublin, where they met Collins, Richard Mulcahy and Cathal Brugha.

Informing them of their plans, the HQ officers suggested a Dublin crew, but the Corkmen insisted that they be the ones to avenge Mac Curtain's murder. They also insisted that the deed be done with Mac Curtain's own gun. They then continued their journey by train to Belfast. With the assistance of the Belfast Brigade, they were successful in their operation and executed Swanzy on his way out of church. Reprisals followed immediately as nationalists and Catholics living in the town and surrounding areas had their homes and businesses burned out.

The Corkmen returned by train to Dublin, where again they were met by Collins, who insisted they hand over their guns, including Mac Curtain's. He said it was for their own safety and promised them they would be returned. Relenting, the men boarded the train for their return journey to Cork.

When the train arrived at Blarney Station, both Culhane and his fellow traveller Dick Murphy decided to leave the train and walk the rest of their way to the city. At Blackpool, both men were stopped and searched at a military checkpoint. After explaining they were only out for a walk, the soldiers allowed them to carry on through. Collins, by insisting they hand over their guns in Dublin, had, in fact, saved their lives.

Tomás Mac Curtain's gun is now on display in the Kilmurray Independence Museum. It was a legally held weapon in its time, and believe it or not, the permit licensing him to hold it was signed off by District Inspector Swanzy. Another former RIC man, Michael Williams, was tracked and captured in county Laois and brought back to Cork. An anonymous letter was sent to his family accusing Martin Corry of torturing Williams at his farm near Knockraha before leaving him to die in agony at the end of a rope. It is now accepted, however, that Corry was not involved. In fact, Williams was court-martialed by the IRA with Sean O'Hegarty as President of the Court and with Tom Crofts and Mrs. Mac Curtain in attendance. He was subsequently found guilty and executed by firing squad.

Sean O'Hegarty was not a blood relation of John Joe, but he and Crofts worked very closely with John Joe, Nan and Mamie. Both used 'The Laurels' as a brigade office and safe house during the War of Independence. When O'Hegarty stepped down as the brigade commanding officer he was succeeded by Tom Crofts. Crofts continued to use it as a meeting place for the duration of the Civil War.

When I spoke to Williams' great-grandnephew Brian (Williams), he informed me his family always believed in his innocence. While Williams admitted being in Cork city that evening, he maintained that he stayed at his sister's house and did not go out. His sister corroborated this alibi. His body has never been discovered.

Gerard Murphy, in his book *The Year Of Disappearances: Political Killings In Cork 1921-22*[3] refers to this event.

3    ISBN 978071714748 9

B. Coy. 1st. Batt.

March 1920.

Lying in State.

Guard of Honour to Lord Mayor McCurtain at Funeral, City Hall.

Sean Culhane.

Matt O'Callaghan.

Liam Coyne.

Arthur White.

Sean O'Sullivan.

D. Corcoran.

"B" Company paraded at funeral as bodyguard.

# The Mitchell Family

Herbert (Seán) Mitchell

Maud Mitchell

Another family that became very involved with all the Hegartys and their activities at 'The Laurels' were Herbert Mitchell (Sean) and his wife, Maud. Both families' lives became intertwined during the War of Independence when Sean used 'The Laurels' as a safe house and went on raids with John Joe.

The Hegarty sisters helped Maud and her young family when Sean was on the run. They also helped her when bringing dispatches and arms to the different columns. Their joint activities continued till the end of the Civil War.

Sean was born in Athlone into a Protestant family in 1891 and was christened Herbert James. He grew up in a very privileged family of planter stock. He became very involved in and committed to the early volunteer movement in Athlone, and he participated in many of its activities. In Easter 1916, he was on his way to join Liam Mellows when the McNeill counter order came not to proceed. When he joined the Volunteers in Cork, he adopted the name Sean.

Not only did it sound more nationalistic, but it would also cover up his very active volunteer service in the Midlands. He became a leading member in the Cork Brigade and was appointed a Captain in 'G' Company by Dick Mulcahy.

Maud (née Mulvihill) was also born in Athlone in 1891 but into a Roman Catholic and nationalist family. Also very active in Athlone and a personal friend of Liam Mellows, she helped him to organise the Midlands Brigade. She was, in fact, the first to be appointed a captain of Cumann na mBan in the Midlands.

# Moving to Cork

Sean was offered a commercial position in Cork which he accepted. Before leaving for Cork, they were presented with a gold medal and brooch by the IRA and Cumann na mBan for their sterling work in the fight for freedom in the Midlands. Both were to continue their total commitment to the cause in Cork from the beginning to the end. Among her many different activities, Maud also became an intelligence officer with 'G' Company in Cork and President of the Bishopstown Cumman na mBan. The Mitchells lived at Clarke's Bridge, College

Road, Glasheen Road, before finally settling permanently in Kerry Pike. In Kerry Pike today, there is a 'Mitchell Court' named after the family, in tribute to their contribution to the cause of Irish independence.

John Joe's Granddaughter Lisa O'Sullivan and her son Ronan Canavan

A book written by her daughter Ruth, *The Man with the Long Hair*, is based on her diary of the times and was not to be published until after her demise. I was privileged to be given a copy by a member of the family.

# Terence MacSwiney, Lord Mayor Of Cork

ᴄᴙᴀᴏʟᴀċ ᴍᴀᴄ ѕᴜɩᵬɴᴇ

Terence MacSwiney

Terence MacSwiney became Mac Curtain's successor both as Brigade Commandant and as Lord Mayor of Cork. In his acceptance speech, he uttered the immortal words regarding the conflict, 'not on our side a rivalry of vengeance, but one of endurance' before declaring, 'it is not they who can inflict the most but they that can suffer most will endure'. Prophetic words that he would shortly put into practice.

The Hegarty's continued their activities under their new commanding officer, whom they knew personally and for whom they had the greatest respect. Whenever his name was spoken in 'The Laurels, it was always with a sense of pride for having served him.

# Burning of RIC Barracks & Tax Office Records

As the war escalated during 1920, Michael Collins issued a decree from Dublin to increase pressure and increase further disruption on the British administration nationwide. This was arranged for early April to coincide with the fourth anniversary of the 1916 Easter Rising.

# Togher Barracks

John Joe with 'H' Company 2nd Batt., together with members of 'G' Company, such as Sean Mitchell, Jeremiah Keating and many of his neighbours, including Joe Murphy, burned their local RIC barracks in Togher. This barracks was situated only a few fields away from 'The Laurels'.

In carrying out this order, Nan was in charge of all the equipment used in the raid. She had the responsibility of returning them all to her home dump on completion of this assignment. She used the gardens of our neighbours and friends the Russells as a shortcut back to The Laurels. Interestingly, years later her brother Patrick married Mary Ellen Russell - the couple had no children. 'The Laurels' was now proving to be, more and more, an important arms depot for the entire Cork Brigade. The order to burn the RIC Barracks was issued to prevent the RIC and/or the Black and Tans from reoccupying them in areas that were now under the control of the IRA; Pouladuff and Togher was one such area.

On the same evening, orders were also given to burn the tax office's records, although not necessarily the buildings. Both of these successful actions resulted in putting a huge financial and logistic strain on the British administration in Ireland.

H. Coy. 2nd. Batt.

<u>Burning of Togher R.I.C. Barracks.</u>

| | |
|---|---|
| Dan Murphy. | Railway Station, Athlone. |
| Edward Barrett. | Lehenagh, Cork. |
| Thomas Leahy. | Greenmount. |
| Jerh. Callanan. | Mt. Merrion Park, Dublin. |
| Con Murphy. | |
| Thomas Collins. | |
| John J. Hegarty. | Pouladuff Rd. |
| Denis Callanan. | 45, Lough Rd., Cork. |
| Jas. Hennessy. | George's Quay, Cork. |
| Chris. Hennessy. | Pouladuff Rd., Cork. |
| Owen Callanan. | St. Finnbarr's Park, Cork. |
| Timy. Hurley. | c/o Sugar Beet Factory, Mallow. |
| Dan Dempsey. | Mental Hospital, Youghal. |
| Con O'Regan. | Blackpool. |
| Jerh. O'Brien. | Clifden Avenue. |
| Con O'Callaghan. | U.S.A. |

# Farran Barracks

On the 21st of June 1920, John Joe was involved in the attack on Farran R.I.C. Barracks, once again with fellow volunteers from 'H' Company, including Joe Murphy, who was to die on hunger strike in Cork Gaol the following October.

A large number of men were involved in the attack. It lasted for over three hours. The sound of explosions and rifle and revolver fire could be heard for miles around. When the RIC reinforcements were dispatched from Cork and Macroom, they were delayed as other volunteers had the roads blocked by trenches and felled trees.

This was an important tactic used many times by the IRA while raids were in progress.

# Railway Raids

During 1920 and 1921, John Joe and his section were also carrying out raids on the Macroom and Capwell railway stations in pursuit of stores. They were also holding up trains on the West Cork railway line. These raids rewarded them with mail that disclosed valuable information on the names and whereabouts of spies who would later be dealt with by the Brigade. They also confiscated bicycles and clothes, which were later given to the members of the columns.

Bicycles were a valuable prize later as they played a pivotal role as a mode of transport for volunteers since vehicles were restricted at the time. Bicycles were an essential asset once the cycle corps was established by the Brigade. This corps acted mainly as scouts prior to engagements, and their vital role in operations is often overlooked. John Joe and his section burned any supplies that were not of use to the Brigade, sending a strong message to the authorities, as well as any future potential spies.

... ... ... Macroom Railway Station (Capwell Station); on several occasions during 1920 & 1921.

| | |
|---|---|
| Edward Barrett. | Lehenagh. |
| Dan Murphy. | Railway Station, Athlone. |
| Jerh. Callanan. | Mount Merrion Park, Dublin. |
| Denis Callanan. | 45, Lough Rd., Cork. |
| John J. Hegarty. | Pouladuff Rd., Cork. |
| Michael Buckley. | Military Barracks, Athlone. |
| Thomas Leahy. | Greenmount, Cork. |
| Patrick O'Connell. | The Lough, Cork. |
| Jas. Hennessy. | George's Quay, Cork. |
| Chris. Hennessy. | Pouladuff Rd., Cork. |
| Thomas Collins. | |
| Dan Dempsey. | Mental Hospital, Youghal. |
| Jerh. O'Brien. | Clifden Avenue. |
| Con O'Regan. | |
| Dan Coveney. | Lehenagh, Cork. |
| Timy. Ahern. | do. |
| Jerh. Connors. | do. |
| T. Donovan. | do. |
| Timy. Hurley. | Sugar Beet Factory, Mallow. |
| Con Foley. | |
| Con O'Callaghan. | U.S.A. |
| Dan Ahern. | do. |
| Charles Harvey. | do. |
| Thos. O'Regan. | The Lough, Cork. |

Railway raids military records

### H. Coy. 2nd. Batt.

Shifting of Company Ammunition from Quartermaster's Dump at
Oliver Plunkett Street during Raid by Auxiliaries.

| | |
|---|---|
| Jerh. Callanan. | Mt. Merrion Park, Dublin. |
| Thomas Leahy. | Greenmount, Cork. |
| Edward Barrett. | Lehenagh, Cork. |
| Denis Callanan. | 45, Lough Rd., Cork. |
| John J. Hegarty. | Pouladuff Rd., Cork. |
| Jas. Hennessy. | George's Quay, Cork. |
| Chris. Hennessy. | Pouladuff Rd., Cork. |

Moving Arms to the Laurels

# Escape From Arms Dump

On one other occasion John Joe, with others from 'H' Company, was shifting a quantity of ammunition from the quartermaster's city centre dump at Oliver

Plunkett Street to 'The Laurels'. What they did not realise was a planned raid by the Auxiliaries was about to commence as they were ready to leave with their stock. Having secured the ammunition, they were lucky to escape with their lives.

John Joe also provided armed guards for the delivery of milk into the city. This became necessary as a number of milkmen had been murdered and their milk supply confiscated by the enemy. At this time, milk was a very important and necessary food supplement for the citizens of Cork.

# Disruptions

The 'H' Company, as with all other companies, made a nuisance of itself by felling trees and digging trenches across many main roads, thus disrupting the transport movement of troops, RIC and Auxiliaries. John Joe was instrumental also in disrupting the British communications network when he and his men took it upon themselves to cut the telephone lines.

# A Touch of Blarney

On one occasion in 1920, prior to her getting married, Mamie, a member of 'H' Company, discovered a rifle and ammunition belonging to a former British soldier while attending the afters of a funeral in Blarney. She swiftly made off with them and with her future husband John, also a member of 'H' Company, delivered them to the arms dump at 'The Laurels'.

# Mamie's Military Wedding

Less than a week after the raid on the Farran Barracks, the family could finally focus solely on the family wedding and honeymoon. The Hegarty siblings by now were all in their early twenties and were all still living at home with their parents.

This all changed on the 26th of June 1920 when Mary Frances married a man by the name of John Forde, a fellow volunteer in 'H' Company.

The wedding of Mary Francis Hegarty and John Forde took place at the Church of the Immaculate Conception, the Lough. The groom, John Forde, was the first to be married in the Irish Volunteers' republican uniform. The bride, who was a President of Cumann na mBan, wore the Old Irish National Wedding Costume, hand-embroidered by the Blackthorn House in Patrick Street.

*Nan Hegarty   Paddy Forde.*
*John Forde,   Mary F. Hegarty.*
*Married in The Lough Church,*
*on 26th June, 1920.*
*By Fr O'Flynn.*

Hegarty family wedding party

Her sister Nan, who herself was a Captain of the Lehenagh Branch of Cumann na mBan, was her bridesmaid, and the best man was Paddy Forde, a cousin of John's who was also a member of the Irish Republican Volunteers. All of their lives were in danger if they were caught, as all were in republican dress.

The ceremony was officiated by Fr. O'Flynn. The church was closed for the ceremony, with sentries posted around the church for their protection. Even on such a joyous family day, John Joe arranged for other members of 'H' Company, including their neighbour Joe Murphy, to provide this necessary protection. It was just a few weeks before the arrest of Lord Mayor Terence MacSwiney and his subsequent hunger strike.

When Joe Murphy was arrested some weeks later and jailed without trial, he also chose to go on hunger strike. The first in the family to get married and to leave home, it must have been an exciting and joyous time for the family, but yet, it did not deter them from their volunteer duties. It had to have been a busy time at 'The Laurels' leading up to the big day. The decision to be married in uniform at such a dangerous time in Cork's history took courage, as did the planning to have armed volunteers in situ to protect them at the service and on their journey by pony and trap to and from the church.

After the ceremony, they all returned to 'The Laurels' to change into civilian clothes and partake of a lavish wedding breakfast that had been arranged by her proud parents. Their decision and determination to have a military wedding had, of course, further endangered the lives of all the family that continued residing at 'The Laurels'.

# Honeymoon

They did not delay too long in 'The Laurels' as they had a train to catch to Youghal in order to begin their honeymoon. John Joe took them to the station, and so they began their married life. On arrival in Youghal, they made their way to the harbour and took the ferry to Ferry Point. On disembarking and by arrangement, they were met by a Mr. Connors with his donkey and cart on which he had two bicycles for them. He took their luggage, and they cycled on to Carty's Cove, where Mamie's good friend Han Roche resided.

The women had become close friends when they were both patients in the North Infirmary Hospital during 1917. Initially, Han couldn't understand the Cork accent and so Mamie had to translate for her.

When the time came for Han to be discharged, she went to 'The Laurels' at the invitation of Mamie's parents to recuperate and shorten her journey as she had to attend outpatients twice weekly. While there, she became part of the family and enjoyed life in the gardens. She also became aware of their subversive activity but fully approved.

The Roches, together with their neighbours, had a lovely celebratory meal prepared for them, allowing them to finally relax before they retired for the night. After the excitement and danger of the day they had in Cork, this new temporary safe haven must have seemed like paradise to the newlyweds. It was a place they would return to often throughout their lives.

When they returned to Cork to begin their new life together, Mamie continued to carry guns, ammunition, and intelligence from Cobh and from her husband John's place of work in the city. Now they were also keeping some at their own at their new home at Greenmount while continuing at times to bring some of them to Mamie's parents' home, further out on the Pouladuff road.

Her new home was also now regarded as a 'call house' for men on their way to the columns and a stopover for Tipperary men such as James Leahy, his future brother-in-law Jack Meagher, and Mick Molloy.

After the Civil War their best man Paddy Forde, like so many other volunteers, emigrated to America where he spent the rest of his life. His son Daniel wrote a book, *A Rebel in the County Cork 1915-1923* based on Paddy's stories. When I asked Dan about the change of spelling of the Forde name he informed me that the Americans could not pronounce Fordeeeeee, so the e was dropped.

My heart I'll give to you

If you'll give yours to me

We'll lock them both
together

And throw away the key.

Joe.

Love note from John to Mamie

# CHURCH OF THE IMMACULATE CONCEPTION
## ST. FINBARR'S WEST, DIOCESE OF CORK

No.

# CERTIFICATE OF MARRIAGE

I HEREBY CERTIFY that it appears by the Marriage Registry of the Parish of ST. FINBARR'S WEST, in the City of Cork, that

*John Forde* and *Mary Frances Hegarty*

were Married according to the Rites of the CATHOLIC CHURCH by the

Rev. *E. O'Flynn*

on the *26th* day of *June* in the year of

Our Lord *Nineteen Hundred & Twenty (1920)*

Names of Witnesses *Patrick Forde & Johanna Hegarty*

Signature of Clergyman *Denis O'Connor C.C.*

Given at Cork this *16th* day of *June* 19*20*

Hickey & Byrne

**Omnibus Quorum Interest Salutem**

Marriage Cert. Military wedding cert.

# A Rebel in the County Cork, 1915-1923 (case study of an insurgency)

*[Here are the opening paragraphs of my 'long essay' about the rebellion that created the Irish Free State and ultimately the Irish Republic. I have suppressed the footnotes. The complete essay can be downloaded as a PDF file from Lulu.com or in the Kindle format for Amazon's e-book reader or the Apple iPhone. Blue skies! -- Dan Ford]*

My father liked to boast that the Irish Republican Army (IRA) invented guerrilla warfare. This was of course a bit of an overstatement. Still, it is indeed the case that, as Andrew Selth argues, the IRA campaign of 1918-1921 'marked the difference between traditional and modern guerrilla warfare', to the extent that it became 'an inspiration and guide to other peoples wishing to change their governments or end colonial rule'.This seems to have been especially true in Asia, where Korean songs were set to Irish tunes, Irish memoirs were translated into Burmese, and India's New Violence Party studied the tactics used in Ireland, where 'some 3,000 insurgents were able to keep a security force of 50,000 at bay for three bitter years'. Indeed, as Ian Beckett concludes, the IRA was 'a true forerunner of modern revolutionary groups in terms of its politically inspired campaign against the British ... though most theorists in the inter-war years failed to recognize it as such'.

In its campaign, the IRA used many of the same tools as 21st century insurgents like Osama bin Laden, from assassination to propaganda aimed at the enemy's population. The outcome, though derided as 'half the loaf' by diehards like my father, seemed to prove that it was 'practical for a relatively small party of fighting revolutionaries to embark on a war against a professional army and that such a war has a fair chance of success'.

Ireland of course was colonized long before India, Burma, or Korea. 'For over seven centuries', writes the British journalist John Kee, 'the history of the people who lived in Ireland had been a folk-trauma comparable in human experience perhaps only to that of the Jews'. It was a history marred by frequent rebellions, usually and foolishly in the form of stand-up fights against the British Army, including most recently the 1916 'Easter Rising' in Dublin—an ill-starred example of Che Gueverra's notion that 'a small group of dedicated

http://www.warbirdforum.com/fordira.htm

Review of best man Paddy Forde's story

# Jailed Without Trial & Hunger Strike

Women waiting outside the gaol (Credit Cork Examiner)

In July and August 1920, only weeks after the wedding, many volunteers were captured and sent to prison without trial. This action by the authorities resulted in a number of them going on a mass hunger strike in Cork Jail.

These prisoners, which included Joe Murphy, were attended to by both Mamie and Nan, as were other Cumann na mBan members, and these young women were able to utilise their first aid knowledge when required.

Nan and Mamie were also busy collecting parcels of goods, including food and cigarettes, for the comfort and well-being of the prisoners who were not on hunger strike. The plight of the hunger strikers gripped the city, with protest slogans such as 'Release the Prisoners' appearing on the walls. Together with Cumann na mBan members, priests and politicians congregated outside the jail in protest.

Some high-profile individuals also visited the prisoners, such as former County Sheriff Mr. P.H. Barry and Dr. Spence, Archbishop of Adelaide. They were appalled at the prisoners' condition. But any protests fell on deaf ears as the British government under its Prime Minister Lloyd George ignored all appeals.

The inaction of authorities was again to give further wider appeal to the IRA cause. When reminiscing about Joe Murphy's hunger strike in jail, Mary O'Leary, his fiancée, told her grandson Teddy Delaney ( a former classmate and teammate of mine in Farranferris) how she used Joe's sister's family pass to gain access to the prison. Brid Kavanagh, another of Mary's grandchildren, also confirmed to me the use of the pass. Mary also told her that she had been given one of Joe's miraculous medals on his demise.

# Death of Hunger Strikers and Funerals

The fact that these prisoners were not given a trial proved to be the catalyst for the strike. Their action was also brought to a wider world audience by a number of American journalists, as one of the strikers, Joe Murphy, had been born there and was, in fact, an American citizen.

On the 25th of October, Joe Murphy, a fellow Volunteer in 'H' Company and the Hegarty's close neighbour and friend, died after seventy-six days on hunger strike. His death is often overshadowed because on the same day, the very popular Lord Mayor of Cork, Terence MacSwiney, died in Brixton Prison London.

In Cork, John Joe removed Joe's body from his cell and the prison itself. Before doing so, he placed the tricolour over Joe's body and then had the lid of the coffin bolted so tightly that the British Army could not have the flag removed as they had previously attempted - although, on that occasion, John Joe also resisted their efforts. He was in charge of the guard of honour when Joe's remains were removed to the family's parish church, the Church of the Immaculate Conception on the Lough Road.

He placed guards there to protect the coffin through the night. This is the same church where Mamie's wedding had taken place just some months previously.

The funeral procession and service were held under the watchful eyes of the British forces, who sought to put restrictions in their way, as the authorities had only allowed 100 people to March behind the coffin.

Despite this, many thousands lined the route from the church to the new republican plot in St Finbarr's cemetery, where he was laid to rest in a coffin of elm. His family instructed the following to be inscribed on the brass plate: 'Brutally done to death by the English in Cork Prison. 25/10/20. Fourth-year of the Republic. In his 24th year. RIP.'

The people of Cork wished to pay their respects to the fallen patriot. When the service was over, John Joe and a party of Joe's fellow volunteers from 'H' Company went back to the cemetery where they fired a volley of shots over his grave as a final salute to their fellow comrade, friend and neighbour. Tensions were running high in the city as a result of the hunger strikers' deaths. Before the strike was called off, three Cork volunteers died at this time, Terence MacSwiney in London, Michael Fitzgerald and Joe Murphy in Cork.

As the Lord Mayor of Cork and the Brigade Commander, MacSwiney was a very popular and important figure to the people of Cork and to the nation as a whole. When his remains were returned to Cork for burial in the republican plot, the streets were lined by thousands, and his death galvanised his followers to strive for independence.

While the service was in progress at the cemetery, the opposite field was occupied by the Black and Tans, who had a piano installed and were playing and singing as a mark of disrespect. They would be singing a different tune before the following year was out.

Michael Fitzgerald, the first Cork hunger striker to die on the 17th of October, was buried not in the republican plot but, by the request of his family, in his family plot at Kilcrumper near Fermoy Co. Cork. He was a commandant in the Cork No 2 Brigade. His early death brought worldwide attention to the plight of the Irish nationalists and their desire for independence. It also brought further tension, fear and anger, not only to the citizens of Cork but also nationally.

The death of MacSwiney resulted in the election of the third republican lord mayor in November 1920, the often overlooked councillor Donal O'Callaghan. He remained Cork's first citizen until January 1924, overseeing a very turbulent time in the city's history.

Teddy Delaney, in his book *Where We Sported And Played*[4] mentions his grandmother Mary O'Leary. Mary married Timothy(Taedy) Owens and had four children. She was widowed at 28 years of age and died aged 86. Fate would have it that in later years her granddaughter Maire Owens would marry Terence MacSwiney's grandson Terence MacSwiney Brugha.

Details of Joe Murphy's funeral

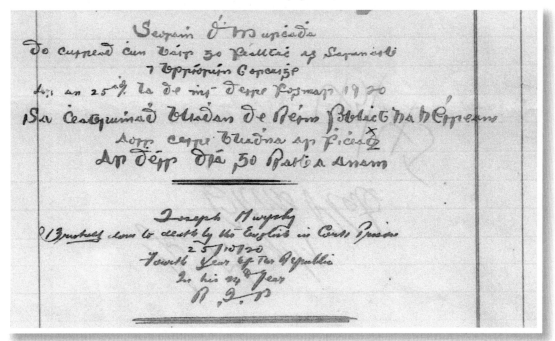

Hegarty Collection

4    ISBN 0 85342 964 2

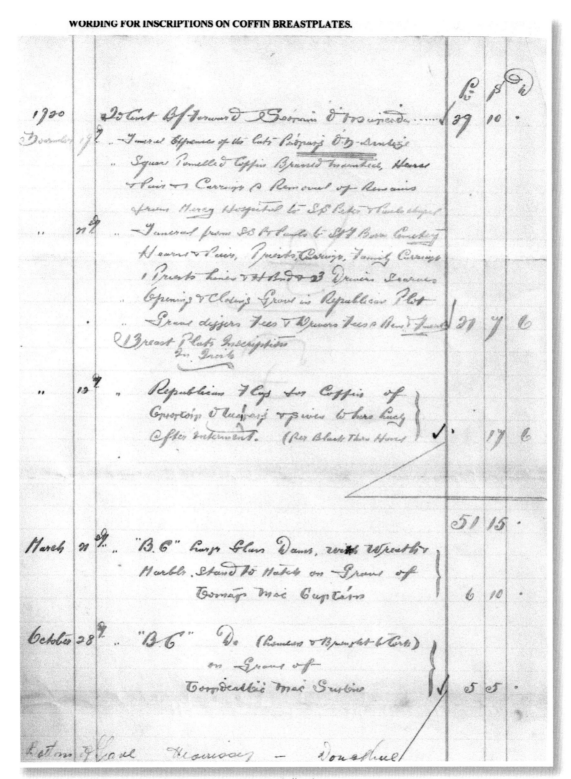

Hegarty Collection

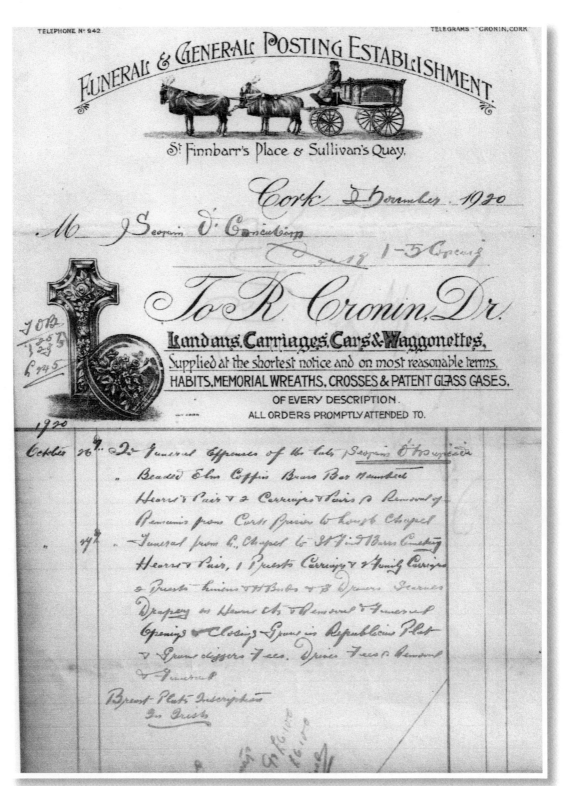

Hegarty Collection

~ 89 ~

Removal of Body of Joseph Murphy (hunger striker) from Cork Gaol
and firing party at Funeral.

| | |
|---|---|
| Edward Barrett. | Lehenagh, Cork. |
| Dan Murphy. | Railway Station, Athlone. |
| Jerh. Callanan. | Mount Merrion Park, Dublin. |
| Owen Callanan. | 45, Lough Rd, Cork. |
| Thomas Leahy. | Greenmount. |
| John J. Hegarty. | Pouladuff Rd. |
| Micheal Buckley. | Military Barracks, Athlone. |
| James Hennessy. | George's Quay. |
| Chris. Hennessy. | Pouladuff Rd. |
| Thomas Collins. | |
| Con O'Callaghan. | U.S.A. |

# Release of Prisoners

When the prisoners were finally released, some were taken to 'The Laurels' in order to recuperate from their ordeal, while others went to Mamie's home for their treatment. There she helped a number of them, including Sean Mitchell, recover their health. One such brave Tipperary man was Sean O'Meara, who, according to his grandniece Breda Kyprianou Nugent, spent more years on the run than in his own home during the struggle. He has the distinction of been a cycle scout at the Soloheadbeg ambush, which triggered the War Of Independence, and was in Dublin when the Four Courts was bombed at the beginning of the Civil War. One of the last to leave, he was at Cathal Brugha's side when Brugha was fatally wounded. After the shooting, Sean was captured and interned by the Free State. He and others wrote momentos in Mamie's autograph album. Jack Meagher recorded the following:

> Some may wish for roses or sweethearts true to be,
> But mine is that old Ireland be freed from Slavery,
> And when that wish is granted when Ireland is free,
> I will die contented, Then Lord take me unto thee.

The Hegartys also attended to Mitchell's wife Maud and their children at her home in Kerry Pike at this time. Consequently, at this time, 'The Laurels' was again targeted by the authorities and raided by the Black and Tans and RIC.

Meanwhile, Jerry O'Brien also confirms that at this time, high-ranking brigade officers were coming and going at 'The Laurels' and that arms and ammunition continued to be stored there. Despite the raids, none were ever detected or confiscated.

Sean Mitchell, when restored to full health in the winter of 1920, arranged to meet Nan at Greenmount school. There he handed her four revolvers, instructing her to bring them to her family home in Pouladuff after he was involved in an attack on Elizabeth Fort on Barrack St. This allowed him to return to his nearby home (at the time at Clarke's Bridge) in the knowledge that the guns were safe as he trusted her and had full confidence in her ability to get things done. It also enabled him to walk home innocently past the Barracks and surrounding area. He also confirms that the siblings' help was invaluable through that year and into 1921 as there were a number of spies in the area who, in his words, 'were properly dealt with'. He had great faith in their tenacity and determination to overcome all obstacles.

Mary O'Leary*                              Joe Murphy*

*Photographed together for the 1st time in over 100 years

# Killingley - Also Known as Killanully

Nan and Mamie also gave a safe haven to men who were on the run at their aunt's and grandparent's property. These were the Walshes, who lived in Killingley near Farmer's Cross, which is on the way to Kinsale. Their home was not only also a safe house, but the nearby 'glen' was used by John Joe, his section, and other volunteer sections as a training ground and a useful place to hold prisoners for interrogation and/or execution. The property later became the family home of Mamie's daughter Eileen and her husband Joe Bowen. The Bowen family were very active during both wars, with Joe's stepbrother Simon being a Captain in F Company 9th Battalion in the Ist Cork Brigade IRA. He worked closely with all the Hegartys during this period. Mamie and Nan had in fact helped to establish the Cumann na mBan branch in the Ballygarvan district. The original house suffered fire damage and burnt down in the 1960's, but was subsequently rebuilt by her brother Hilary's building firm. The property remains in the ownership of the Forde family.

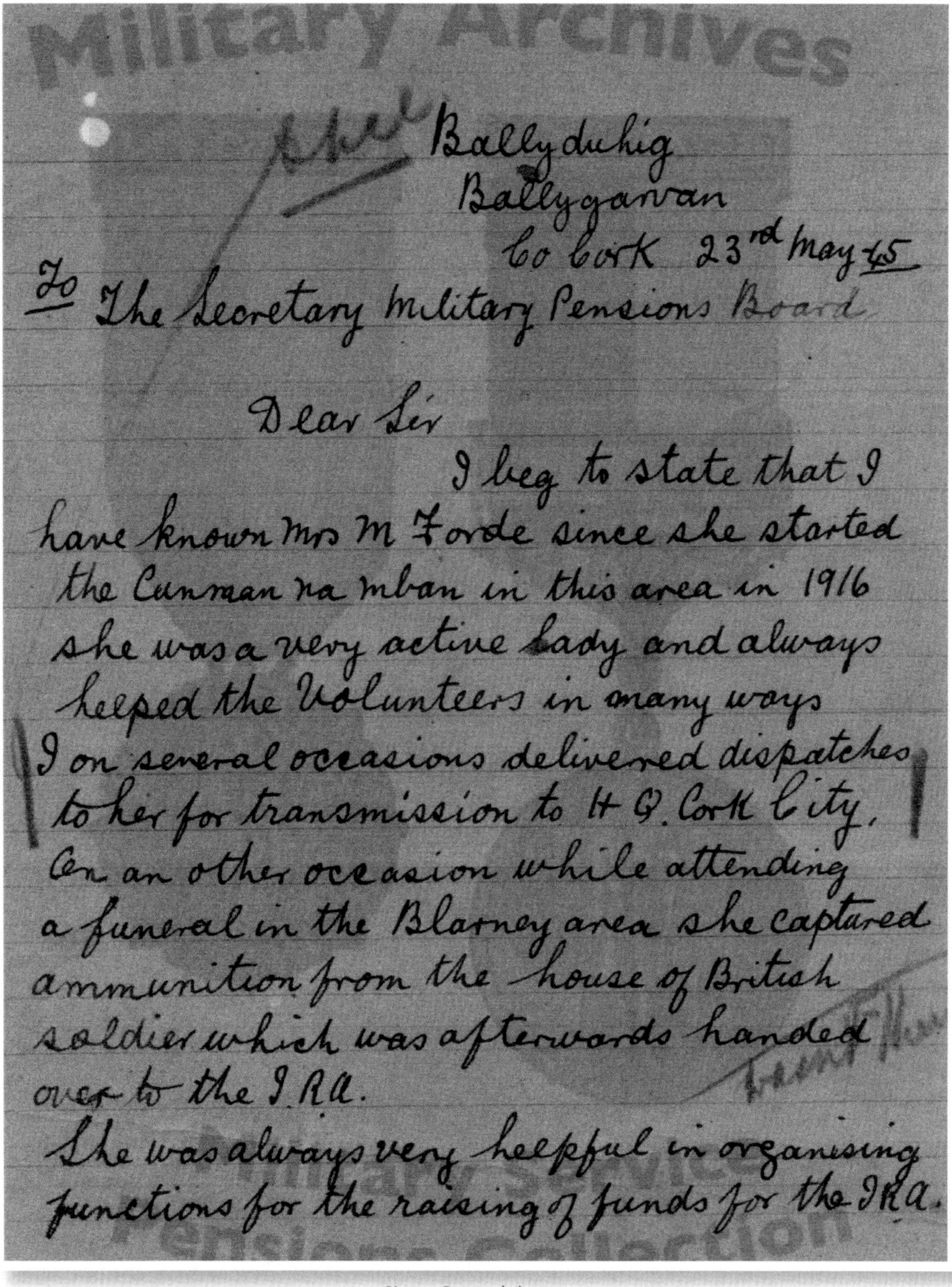

Ballyduhig
Ballygarvan
Co Cork 23rd May 45

To The Secretary Military Pensions Board

Dear Sir

I beg to state that I
have known Mrs M Forde since she started
the Cumann na mban in this area in 1916
she was a very active lady and always
helped the Volunteers in many ways
I on several occasions delivered dispatches
to her for transmission to H Q. Cork City.
On an other occasion while attending
a funeral in the Blarney area she captured
ammunition from the house of British
soldier which was afterwards handed
over to the I.R.A.
She was always very helpful in organising
functions for the raising of funds for the I.R.A.

Simon Bowen's letter

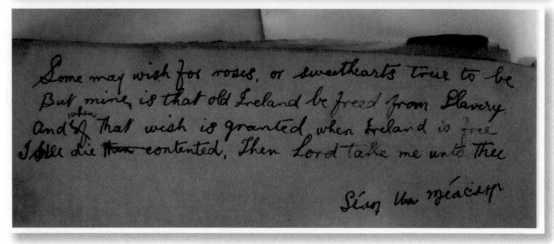

I can honestly state that both herself and her husband R.I.P. were leading lights in the Cumman na mban and IRA.

Signed.

Simon Bowen

Capt F Company 9th Battallion 1st Cork Brigade IRA.

Some may wish for roses, or sweethearts true to be But mine, is that old Ireland be freed from Slavery. And if that wish is granted when Ireland is free I die contented, Then Lord take me unto thee

Seán Ua Meachair

John Meagher's note to Mamie

# Munitions Strike

The IRA got more support during 1920 when the Cork dock workers refused to offload any British military equipment. When they were joined by the railway workers, it became known as the year of the 'munitions strike'. Their strikes were fully supported by the Irish Transport and General Workers Union, and their actions were a major contributor to the British government's declaration of martial law in the city.

This law allowed the military to carry out reprisals against the general population and to execute anyone who was arrested carrying arms. This new law put both Nan's and

Mamie's life in more danger, but it did not prevent them from carrying arms around the city after curfew. Movement on the streets during the hours of darkness was banned every night, and householders had to post on their doors the names and personal details of all occupants. If others not listed were found on the property, it was deemed an illegal gathering and those present were arrested or attacked or both, and the property was more than likely ransacked. 'The Laurels' as a 'call' or 'safe' house put all of the Hegartys in real danger.

# Excommunication

In December 1920, the Catholic Bishop of Cork, Rev. Daniel Cohalan, in his wisdom, decided in the public interest to excommunicate all IRA members. This despite the fact that very many priests in the diocese supported their cause. Priests such as Fr. Dominic O'Connor, who was in fact appointed chaplin to the Cork Brigade by Mac Curtain, was one of the first people to appear at his home on the morning of his murder.

It was also the month the Black and Tans went on the rampage and burned Cork city centre after an attack on Auxiliaries as they left Victoria Barracks. The attack left 12 people injured, one of whom died later. By the end of the year, the people of Cork had to come to terms with the death of two republican lord mayors. This, combined with martial law, a curfew, and the publication of the findings pertaining to the Kilmichael ambush, created an atmosphere of fear for all its citizens.

The bishop's decision and the authority's reign of terror did not deter the Volunteers in their quest for freedom. In fact, it made them even more determined to succeed with growing support from the public.

# Martial Law, 1921-22

'The Laurels,' despite martial law having been imposed, continued as a very important arms dump for the full Cork Brigade. Men such as Liam Og O'Callaghan, P. O'Sullivan and Charles O'Connell, all of 'D' Company, continued to move rifles and arms for the brigade column from the dump developed in Fairfield on the northside of the city to 'The Laurels' under John Joe's total control in Pouladuff.

Raids began early in the new year. John Joe supplied revolvers and ammunition for the Parnell Bridge ambush on the evening of the 4th of January 1921. A party of ten RIC men were returning to Union Quay Headquarters, which was then the main police barracks in the city. As they crossed Parnell Bridge, they came under gun and bomb attack by members of the 1st Battalion of Cork, No 1 Brigade. Six RIC men were wounded, with two dying of their injuries later.

January 1921. Moving Arms for Brigade Column.

This was during Martial Law. The following members of the Company moved rifles from the Company Dump at the Fair Field to John Joe Hegarty's house.

Liam Og O'Callaghan
P. O'Sullivan.
Charles O'Connell.

Limerick.
9, St. Mary's Tce., Fair Hill.
2, St. Vincent's Place. Blarney St.

D Company military record

This was a very active time for the IRA in Cork, and 'H' Company was not shy in playing its part. John Joe was now also responsible for guarding the brigade officer Sean O'Hegarty, who was staying at 'The Laurels,' all of this time with the blessing and approval of his parents.

# Ambushes

'H' Company was now also transporting arms and ammunition to Gurrane for the brigade column. Gurrane is a townland of the large parish of Innishannon, which is close to Crossbarry, Ballincollig, Upton and Killumney. There were a number of well-documented ambushes at that time, notably on the 15th of February at Upton under the command of Charlie Hurley. Hurley was a much-respected officer and demonstrated his leadership qualities during this particular ambush by continuing to fight on despite being severely wounded

# Coolavokig

There was another ambush on the 25th of February at Coolavokig near Ballyvourney, under the command of Sean O'Hegarty. It is reported that this was one of the biggest battles recorded at the time. The Crown forces based in Macroom were on a rounding-up exercise. As they travelled towards Ballyvourney, they ran into the ambush, which had been very well prepared. The attack lasted two hours. They had to fight a rearguard action all the way back to Macroom, which they then put on lockdown.

Reinforcements were rushed from Cork, Ballincollig and other nearby barracks. They scoured the surrounding district making arrests, confining people to their homes, and recovering their dead. In the aftermath, a number of the volunteers, now 'on the run', made their way to 'The Laurels,' which was a safe place that was familiar to O'Hegarty.

There they were attended to by Nan and the family. They were fed and washed, their wounds were attended to, and they were given a place to rest. There they disposed of their weapons when heading home or conversely rearmed before heading back to the column.

Conveyance of Arms and Ammunition to Gurrane for Brigade Column.

| | |
|---|---|
| Edward Barrett. | Lehenagh, Cork. |
| Jerh. Callanan. | Mt. Merrion Park, Dublin. |
| John F. Hegarty. | Pouladuff Rd, Cork. |
| Dan Murphy. | Railway Station, Athlone. |
| Thomas Collins. | Curragh Rd. |
| Denis Callanan. | 45, Lough Rd, Cork. |
| Jas. Hennessy. | George's Quay, Cork. |
| Chris. Hennessy. | Pouladuff Rd., Cork. |
| Dan Dempsey. | Mental Hospital, Youghal. |
| Con O'Regan. | Blackpool. |
| Thomas Leahy. | Greenmount, Cork. |

# Crossbarry

Prior to the Crossbarry ambush, Nan was actively engaged in intelligence work for Tom Barry's column, a force of between 80 and 100 men. This ambush occurred on the 19th of March when the column escaped encirclement by over a thousand British troops and Auxiliaries. On one occasion, Nan was lucky to escape a raid by the military just as she brought arms to Crossbarry. It was during this ambush that the patriot Charlie Hurley was mortally wounded. 'The Laurels' continued to be used as an arms dump and bomb factory while John Joe and the rest of 'H' Company continued to hold up trains and to capture goods on their way to Ballincollig Barracks. They also raided Macroom Railway Station for mail and supplies.

Excommunicating the IRA did not spare the life of Fr James O'Callaghan, the very popular curate in Clogheen and a former pupil of Farranferris. He was murdered in cold blood by the RIC in May while staying at the home of Liam deRoiste TD, in Sunday's Well.

On the 24th of June, John Joe was active as one of the covering party when Tuckey St RIC Barracks was raided, and he brought back arms after the attack. The intelligence work and the other brave activities of John Joe, Nan and Mamie helped in no small way to bring the War of Independence to an end.

Their teamwork and support for one another more than likely accounts for both their success and, indeed, their very survival. The support, encouragement, and approval of their parents Patrick and Elizabeth, must also be acknowledged during this dangerous time in our history.

Patrick and Elizabeth Hegarty

Nan's notes to Mamie on survival

# Truce

Éamon de Valera

Michael Collins

De Valera insisted on a truce as a condition before any negotiating of a Treaty between Ireland and Britain. After the ceasefire and subsequent truce were announced and ratified on the 11th of July 1921, one of the last fatal actions of the war took place in Cork. A number of British soldiers left their (jail) barracks prior to the appointed time and were seen walking up the nearby Bandon Road.

When this was brought to the attention of some volunteers attending a function in Father O'Leary's Hall, also on the Bandon Road, they overpowered the soldiers and executed them. They dumped their bodies in the Ellis Quarry, which was located near the Lough. They were deliberately only discovered the following day.

The London government was fuming and insisted that Dublin should bring those responsible to account, and they should be punished for their actions. It fell to Conn Neenan, the local officer, to establish who was responsible and on completion of his task to report back to Michael Collins at HQ in Dublin.

Two of the executed soldiers were from the South Staffordshires, a regiment that was notorious for their dealings with and killing of prisoners they held, particularly unarmed volunteers and civilians. The official reason for the killings was always 'trying to escape from military capture'. The other two soldiers were from the Royal Engineers. There had been a number of recent killings by the Staffordshires, and slogans had been daubed on walls in the city: 'Murdered by the Stafford Regt - Will be revenged tonight.'

A volunteer Denis Spriggs had been murdered by them just a few days earlier. Spriggs was given a military funeral, and he is buried in the republican plot.

# Meeting At Barr's Club

Per instructions, Conn called a meeting of the local Volunteers and Cumann na mBan members in the old Barr's club and told the assembled gathering that he had been ordered by HQ to find out who was responsible for killing the soldiers and to report this back to Dublin.

Nan told me that John Joe put it to Conn that if he was responsible for reporting back to Dublin the names of those who shot the soldiers, who did he think would be responsible for relaying news of his shooting. Needless to say, that was the end of any reporting. There was no further discussion, and the meeting ended. When I had the opportunity to ask Conn about this story, he just smiled and nodded in the affirmative. It is ironic that the finger was always pointed at Conn for ordering these executions, something he always denied. It is accepted, however, that it was local volunteer members who were responsible for the killings.

Shooting of Four British Soldiers on Eve of the Truce

# The Capture of the Upnor - A Naval Battle

In March 1922, just months prior to the commencement of the Civil War, the IRA, under the command of Sean O'Hegarty, whose planning and intelligence work was second to none, launched an audacious plot to secure arms. This raid was not to take place in the city or county of Cork but rather off its coast. Hegarty became aware that a British vessel, the 'Upnor,' was to transport arms and ammunition from the soon-to-be decommissioned Haulbowline base back to the UK.

Mamie and her husband John helped in obtaining much of the intelligence as he was free to roam Cobh and had access to enemy positions as their official undertaker. When Hegarty had sufficient information, he summoned Michael Burke, Commander of the Cobh IRA, informing him of the plan to capture the 'Upnor' at sea and take her to Ballycotton, where the Cork Brigade would unload its contents and arrange transport back to the city. Burke was to make contact with his men in Haulbowline and to let him know in advance when the 'Upnor' was ready to leave.

When word came to him that the ship was ready to sail, Burke contacted Hegarty, and the plan was set in motion. Brigade officers Tom Crofts, Mick Murphy and 'Sando Donovan, together with other volunteers, left Cork and travelled to Cobh. They also brought with them Captain Collins, a civilian with naval experience who had been helpful to the brigade on previous occasions. In his book *For the Life of Me*[5] Robert Briscoe describes how Collins had previously sold the IRA's gun-running tugboat the 'Frieda' at a profit to His Majesty's Navy in Cobh as a coal boat.

In Cobh, a tugboat, 'The Warrior,' was secured and its captain held prisoner in Cobh so he could not raise the alarm. With everything in order, they set out to pursue the 'Upnor' after it left Cork Harbour, despite the fact it was to be escorted by two naval battleships (HMS. Heather and Strenuous).

The battleships were sailing about three miles in front of the 'Upnor,' as was normal navy practice. Everything went to plan under the command of Michael Murphy. The ship was boarded about thirty-five miles off the coast after the ship's captain accepted the story that a private tug, the 'Warrior,' was carrying a message from the Admiralty.

On boarding the 'Upnor,' the captain at gunpoint protested this act of piracy, but he and his crew put up no resistance. Then under the control of the IRA, and with its own crew now on board, Captain Collins was instructed to change course and head for Ballycotton. The warships acting as escorts, meanwhile, were unaware of its change of course.

5    Congress Catalog 58-10683

Photo of Upnor

# Capturing the Arms

In Ballycotton, the IRA unloaded its substantial cargo of arms. Waiting on the quays were members of Cork IRA with lorries that were 'borrowed' earlier from around the city to transport them back to Cork. Anti-Treaty officers such as Martin Corry and his men helped to unload its substantial cargo of arms. Mamie was in charge of organising the Cumann na mBan for this operation. She was familiar with Ballycotton, having established a branch there some years earlier. She helped to carry arms back to Cork. Some found their way to her home in Greenmount and others to her parent's home, 'The Laurels' in Pouladuff. More were brought to Kerry Pike, now the home of Sean and Maud Mitchell, who had participated in the raid and the seizure of the arms.

It is generally reported that all unnecessary goods on board such as chairs and desks were abandoned at the quayside in Ballycotton. However, a supply of blue nurses' uniforms were later discovered during the Civil War when the Mitchell's home and premises were raided by Free State troops.

The vast majority of the arms were dispatched to West Cork locations which were then under the control of the IRA anti-Treaty forces. It was, in fact, the first and only naval conflict between Ireland and Britain. The British government was fuming and saw this as an act of piracy and a breach of the truce. Michael Collins, on the other hand, blamed the Admiralty under Winston Churchill for attempting to undermine the Provisional Government.

Collins was aware of the political uncertainty that was prevalent in Cork regarding the terms of the truce. Either way, this daring operation supplied the Cork IRA with plenty of arms, ammunition and mines for the imminent Civil War.

Back in Cobh the following morning, Burke was summoned to the Admiralty and asked if he knew anything about the event. He told them he had no knowledge of it and returned to his home aware of their inferior intelligence.

In London, Winston Churchill, as Secretary Of State for the Colonies had to report the event to his government and account for his stewardship.

In the House of Commons, Churchill was questioned by John Robert Newman MP, a Cork-born British Army officer and Conservative politician. Newman received his commission in the 5th Battalion, Royal Munster Fusiliers. He had formerly been Deputy Lieutenant and Justice of the Peace for Cork County, as well as serving as the county's High Sheriff in 1898. All in all, he was a man unimpressed with events in his native county and country.

# Churchill Reports to the House Of Commons

The House of Commons record of Newman's exchange with Winston Churchill reads:

*In early April, Colonel Newman asked The President of the Board of Trade whether his attention has been called to the capture of a British-owned tug by supposed members of the Irish Republican Party at Queenstown; its disappearance to sea and subsequent recapture by the naval sloop 'Heather'; has he any reasons to give for the occurrence, and to whom have these found on board the tug and not members of the crew been handed over for custody?*

*The Secretary of State for the Colonies (Mr. Churchill) replied:*

Winston Churchill

*I must ask the indulgence of the house to permit me to make a full answer to this question. The facts of this incident have appeared in an exaggerated form. The vessel in question (the Upnor) contained over 400 rifles and not 20,000, as I have seen stated. There were in addition 700 revolvers and 39 machine guns, about half a million rounds of rifle ammunition, and certain other naval stores, including a small quantity of explosives.*

*These munitions were being transported by the Admiralty from Haulbowline Dockyard to Devonport in the usual way. The 'Upnor' was piratically captured upon the high seas by a gang of Republican conspirators hostile to the Provisional Government who had previously seized a tug in Queenstown Harbour. The 'Upnor' was taken to Ballycotton, about ten or fifteen miles from*

*Queenstown, where the greater part of the arms and ammunition on board were unloaded. At the same time, about a hundred motor lorries were commandeered by the anti-Treaty Republicans in Cork and brought to Ballycotton Bay with several hundred men. The arms and ammunition stolen from the 'Upnor' were removed in these lorries, about sixty of which returned empty.*

*As soon as the British naval authorities were aware of what was taking place, one Of His Majesty's ships proceeded in search of the 'Upnor' and found her in Ballycotton Bay. The Republican raiders had dispersed on the news of the British warship leaving Queenstown, but the local population was engaged in looting the contents of the vessel.*

*The incident is a very serious one. It constitutes a gross and dishonorable breach of the truce. I must remind the house that the truce was entered into, not with the Provisional Government alone, but with the duly elected representatives of the Irish people, who were and are parties to it. The fact that such an elaborate conspiracy could be set on foot in Cork without the Provisional Government obtaining any previous or even early information of it shows that their control over Cork and this district is practically non-existent. This is all the more remarkable in a city in which opinion has overwhelmingly declared itself on the side of the Treaty.*

*I am communicating with the Provisional Government in this sense. At the same time, I am bound to admit that an inalienable responsibility rests upon the British government to safeguard in all circumstances arms and ammunition of war that are in their hands. The Admiralty are instituting an inquiry into the circumstances, with a view to ascertaining whether any neglect of reasonable precautions has occurred, and I need scarcely say that naval escorts will be employed in future in regard to all movements of munitions from Ireland by sea.*

As the above illustrates, the British Parliament was not impressed by this daring raid. It did once again however highlight how effective the IRA's intelligence network was and also its planning and attention to detail. Not only did they succeed in concealing the planning of this operation from the British, but also from the Free State authorities.

Both the 'official' crews from the Warrior and the Upnor were immediately arrested after the event and taken into custody in Queenstown. They all were questioned about the event but were subsequently found not guilty of any involvement and released without charge.

# Pre-Civil War

Just prior to the Civil War, Sean O'Hegarty, who strongly opposed the Treaty, took a neutral stance and tried to broker a deal in order to avoid outright war between both sides. He made his decision at the same meeting that James Leahy attended when Leahy decided to cut short his honeymoon and return to Tipperary when he was informed of the bombing of the Four Courts.

Seamus Leahy informed me that on one occasion, Sean travelled to Rathmines Dublin, to the home of Richard Mulcahy, the then Commanding Officer of the Free State Army, only to be told by him to get off his property as he considered him a coward for not taking one side or the other.

Years later when this story was related by Seamus to Michael Joseph Costelloe, a former IRA intelligence officer and later a Lieutenant General in the Irish Army, Costelloe, without raising his eyes, replied, 'Sean O'Hegarty may be accused of many things, but cowardice was NOT one of them'.

Hegarty's personal stance on neutrality mirrors that taken by hundreds of other volunteers. Costelloe, who was a native of Cloughjordan, took the Treaty side during the Civil War. His godfather was Thomas MacDonagh, also from Cloughjordan, a signatory to the Proclamation of the Irish Republic. For his role in the 1916 Easter Rising on the 3rd of May 1916, he was executed along with Thomas Clarke and Padraig Pearse. MacDonagh wrote the poem 'The Man Upright' in 1911/12, inspired by the behaviour and actions of Costelloe's father Denis, his friend, a fellow school teacher, and a man known to never bow his head to anyone.

# 'The Man Upright'

I once spent an evening in a village

Where the people are all taken up with tillage,

Or do some business in a small way

Among themselves, and all the day,

Go crooked, doubled to half their size,

Both working and loafing, with their eyes

Stuck in the ground or in a board,

For some of the tailor, and some of the hoard

Pence in a till in their little shops,

And some of the shoe- soles - they get the tops

Ready-made from England, and they die cobblers-

All bent up double, a village of hobblers

And slouchers and squatters, whether they struggle

Up and down, or bend to haggle

Over a counter, or bend at a plough,

Or to dig with a spade, or to milk a cow,

Or to shove the goose - iron stiffly along

The stuff on the sleeve- board or lace the fong

In the boot on the last, or to draw the wax-end

Tight cross-ways - and so to make or to mend

What will soon be worn out by the crooked people

The only thing straight in the place was the steeple,

I thought at first, I was wrong in that

For there past the window at which

I sat Watching the crooked little men

No slouching, and with a gait of a hen

An odd little woman go pattering past,

And The cobbler crouching over his last

In the window opposite, and next door

The tailor squatting inside on the floor--

While I watch them, as I have said before,

And thought that only the steeple was straight

There came a man of a different gait--

A man who neither slouched nor pattered,

But planted his steps as if each step mattered;

Yet walk down the middle of the street

Not like a policeman on his beat,

But like a man with nothing to do

Except walk straight upright like me and you.

Tómas MacDonagh

MacDonagh highlighted the negative effects of British imperial rule on the Irish Nation. Calling for its people to stand tall and free.

# Treaty

The Articles of Agreement for a Treaty between Great Britain and Ireland were signed on the 21st of December 1921. This resulted in rallies being organised nationwide to garner support for its acceptance. Many were disrupted with speakers not allowed to speak, shots fired, and meetings broken up by anti-Treaty supporters. After one such rally in Cork, attended by John Joe, fellow Brigade members and supporters, Maud Mitchell reports that her husband Sean went to see Michael Collins in Moore's Hotel. Collins offered Sean the position of Command of the Southern Division of the Free State Army. Sean queried Mick saying, 'You don't mean to split the Army?' 'To hell with the Army,' replied Collins. Sean retorted, 'Well, to hell with you.'

The stage was set for outright Civil War.

# Civil War

On the 28<sup>th</sup> of June 1922, the Free State army opened fire on the republican headquarters based in the Four Courts, Dublin. At the outbreak of the Civil War, unlike many families, there were no divided loyalties in the Hegarty household. John Joe, Mami, Nan and family all took the anti-Treaty side, and they continued their activity as intelligence officers and arms suppliers. Sean O'Hegarty, having stepped down, was replaced by Tom Crofts as Commanding Officer of the anti-Treaty IRA, and Crofts continued to visit and use 'The Laurels' as a meeting place on a regular basis for the remainder of the Civil War.

During this period, John Joe continued to make landmines and arms at 'The Laurels'. The house was now being used not only by IRA brigade officers but also by men on the run who used it as a call house on a daily basis when going to and from the columns. Simultaneously Mamie's home in Greenmount was being used by prominent members of the IRA for the same purpose. When, for example, Elizabeth Fort, Barrack Street was captured, many of the arms came from the supply dump at 'The Laurels'.

# Dan Breen's
# APPEAL

### Dan Breen's Appeal to His Old Comrades now in the Free State Army.

## COMRADES!

Are you aware that you are fighting against the Republic that you fought to establish in 1916, and that was maintained and is going to be maintained?

Are you aware that England tried to disestablish the Republic through a reign of Black and Tan terror?

Are you aware that she is now using the so-called Provisional Government to try where she failed?

Are you aware that YOU are the Black and Tans of to-day, the only difference is the uniform?

Are you aware that the death of CATHAL BRUGHA is a damnable and eternal stain on the uniform?

Are you aware that CATHAL BRUGHA died as my comrade, SEAN TREACY, died?—no surrender to the enemies of the Republic was their cry.

Are you aware that there are hundreds of MEN who will die as Brugha and Treacy died in defence of the Republic?

Are you aware that I did my best to maintain the army for the Republic, but I failed because your section took orders from our only enemy—England?

Comrades, I thought my term of soldiering was over, but duty has again called me to defend the Republic, which I will do or die in the attempt.

Will you again stand with me as my comrades in arms, or will you continue to fight with England against me?

### DAN BREEN

Dan Breen's Appeal

# The Irish Free State

'The Laurels' continued to be raided, but now it was the turn of Free State troops. On one particular occasion, a motorcycle was taken away. This they knew had been used for delivering dispatches and ammunition during the War of Independence and was now suspected of being used for similar activities during the Civil War. It was never returned.

During this period, John Joe was busy dividing his time moving arms and ammunition for his section and his column's use. He continued to gather intelligence in the city. He was involved in an attack against Free State troops at the Viaduct Bridge and also came under fire from troops as he was delivering despatches.

The intelligence he was collecting was very important and could be relied on by the Brigade, so much so his commanding officer Sean Mitchell recognised its importance and ordered him to concentrate on this essential activity.

He was now handing over arms concealed at the dump at 'The Laurels' for men of the column and finding safe houses for those operatives on the run, operatives who came into the locality, some escaping from jail and so forth. This was no easy task as the whole area was bitterly hostile. He again wanted to rejoin the column full-time, but this request was refused. The Brigade Intelligence Officer was adamant that he was much more useful in the city than in the county as the reports received from him could not be secured from any other source. This resulted in his giving all his time to Intelligence work and neglecting his home and family business.

# Free State Troops Land in Cork

On the 8th of August 1922, Free State troops landed at Passage resulting in heavy fighting taking place, particularly in the Rochestown area as anti-Treaty troops tried to stop their advance on the city. Heavily outnumbered, the anti-Treaty side (IRA) was forced to withdraw.

It must be remembered that Free State troops were bolstered by many former volunteers who were now being paid for the first time by the state. While retreating, six of the injured men made their way to Greenmount and to the

home of Mamie, where she washed and fed them and treated their wounds before escorting them out of the city to Ballincollig. Men such as Sean Mitchell and Jerry O'Brien also went to her home at that time.

Nan, John Joe and their parents were also attending to men on the run, providing them with shelter at 'The Laurels' and supplying them with arms from their arms dump. Meanwhile, John Joe continued his intelligence work, helping the IRA with all its activities.

Nan and Mamie were also looking after the Mitchell family by bringing them food and supplies, and treats for the children. On one particular occasion when Nan was there, the house was raided by Free State troops, with shots fired over it to scare the occupants. Nan also minded the Mitchell children when their house was the venue for brigade meetings.

She also accompanied Maud on visits to the ASU and took arms to Sean while he was operating in the 3rd Brigade area. Some days later, the IRA abandoned the city and burned all the barracks they were occupying.

When the IRA was abandoning Templemore Barracks in Tipperary, some of James Leahy's group were about to burn it, so the Free Staters wouldn't get it. Leahy ruled the other way after travelling to Carrick-on-Suir to link up with de Valera, making the case 'better that Tipperary have the Barracks than it be lost'. After much deliberation, Dev agreed to his request. The Barracks is now named after the local dead patriot

Pierce McCan. McCan was a close friend of Cathal Brugha.This retreat allowed John Joe to go back 'on the run' with the column.

Ironically, in later years Mamie and her husband John Forde established their family undertaking business and home in the shadows of Fort Elizabeth, Barrack Street, one of the barracks they helped to burn. Nan's son, Gus Fennell, also set up his garage business on Frenches Quay. He also spent a lot of his time and enjoyed many meals at 'The Laurels', where he also inherited a love of greyhounds. Both their businesses were under the protection and watchful eye of the Garda barracks. The Fort is now one of Cork city's main tourist attractions.

Forde Family: Teddy, Hilary, Eileen, Lily, Paddy and Dee

Nan with Dee Forde and his children Mary Frances and John

CUPS PRESENTED—Miss M. Lyons, centre on left, presents her father's trophy to Mr. M. C. O'Leary, who received it on behalf of Mrs. W. D. Darrer, owner Killeens, winner of the Sunday League and Cup at Dromina, Co. Cork. On right, Mr. J. Cashman presents his cup to Mr. G. Fennell, owner of the winner.

Gus Fennell being presented with coursing trophy and Jim with the winning dog 'Warrington Lass' 1960s. Credit Cork Examiner.

# Arrest of John Joe

At the height of the Civil War in December 1922, while 'on the run', John Joe's luck ran out when he was arrested in Cork city while on intelligence work and charged with being an intelligence officer for the IRA. He was also questioned about Sean Mitchell, his commanding officer, who at that time was staying at 'The Laurels' with the expectation that he would remain there over the Christmas period.

They threatened to shoot John Joe if he did not surrender Mitchell. John Joe was also questioned about the whereabouts of any bomb factories and dumps under his control. His life was saved when a Free State officer recognised him and arranged for his release. It may have been this action that influenced John Joe to believe in the importance of reconciliation in later years.

It is documented that 300 anti-Treaty prisoners nationwide were released on the 23rd as a clemency gesture by the Free State Government. Many anti-Treaty prisoners were selected and murdered during the period of the Civil War as a reprisal for other murders. Today these tit-for-tat murders would more than likely be treated as war crimes.

## Period 6

I raided Military Goods train enroute
to Ballincollig Barracks at Bishopstown. Burning
all supplies. I was in charge of dump which
was located on my premises. I supplied
Revolvers & Ammunition to men who took part
in the Parnells Bridge Ambush, and
guarded the Brigade O/C. who was staying
in my House.

In xmas 1922 I was arrested
in Cork City while on Intelligence work. I
was accused of being an I.O. and was questioned
regarding a prominent I.R.A. man "Sean Michel"
who had been staying in my house during
the week. I was threatened to be shot if I did
not devulge his whereabouts, and the dump which
I was in charge of. This would probably have
happened but for the intervention of a I.S. Officer
whom I knew, and who later had me released

I was fired on by. I.S. troops while
riding Motor Cycle carrying dispatches. I asserted

~ 120 ~

In the attack on I. S. Soldiers at the Vadnul Bridge and gave information about I.I troops who were afterwards attacked in Barrack A.

I again tried to go away in column but the Brigade I.O. refused to allow me saying that I was much more useful in the City than in the Country as reports received from me could not be got from any other source.

During this period I gave all my time to Intelligence Work neglecting both my home & business. I was responsible for a dump of arms which was concealed on my place, On different occasions I had to received hand over Rifles to men going to & from Columns.

My work consisted of finding safe billet for men badly wanted who came into the locality, men escaping from Jail etc.. This was no easy job. as the whole district was bitterly hostile.

J. J. Hegarty

John Joe's letter

# Post-War

When the war was over, John Joe worked in the market gardens full-time with his father and continued to bring their produce to the city markets and shops daily. Men and women workers spent long hours there, as it was labour intensive planting, weeding and eventually harvesting the crops. All plants grown in the garden came from seeds that were harvested on an annual basis and stored in the sheds, thus enabling a supply of plants in perpetuity.

Basic meals were provided, and, just as important, a dry privy was built in the garden that needed managing on a regular basis. A similar facility was attached to the main house. This situation continued until local housing development began in the sixties and access to the main sewage was provided. The main mode of transport was by horse and cart, which was still in use up to the mid-sixties, at such time a van was purchased. It must have been around this time that John Joe, as the second son, began to consider his future as a single man in the Free State.

When I was a young boy, I remember one of John Joe's gardeners, David (Davy) Leary, and former member of 'H' Company, telling me that he had taken the Treaty side when the Civil War broke out and that in at least one ambush he and John Joe had exchanged rifle fire on opposite sides. When the war was over, John Joe approached him, saying, "Davy, your job is still there if you would like to return to work at 'The Laurels.'" Two friends and former foes reconciled for life.

Incidentally, for years as a child, I thought we had de Valera working in the gardens!

# Fianna Fáil

In 1926 Fianna Fáil was founded. John Joe and the family became interested and joined the party, becoming strong supporters of Martin Corry, a former comrade, and a founding member. Martin's mother and John Joe's mother were both related through the Walsh side of their families.

Martin was elected a Fianna Fáil Teachta Dala (TD) in the June 1927 general election. He has the distinction of being returned a TD at every election until he stood down at the 1969 general election. During the War of Independence, Corry acted as a senior member of the Cork No 1 Brigade and their 'chief executioner,' responsible for multiple killings of soldiers, RIC members and spies. His prisoners were brought to a place of execution known as 'Sing Sing' and were never seen again. This is something he never denied, including in an interview shortly before he died.

In the 1930s, his opposition to the Blueshirts almost resulted in his home being burned down. The Blueshirts (The Army Comrades Association) were founded in the early 1930s when tensions were running high on a political level both at home and on mainland Europe. They provided physical protection from intimidation and attack by the anti-Treaty (IRA) to political groups such as

Cumann na nGaedheal. Most of these groups later merged to become Fine Gael. Even today, members of this party are still at times referred to as Blueshirts.

Nan's grandson Emmet Fennell
at the entrance to 'Sing Sing'

Emmet Fennell with
children Tom and
Anna at the Corry
Homestead

# Hit Squad

When I became interested in this period of history, I always wanted to ask John Joe if he was responsible for the detection and elimination of soldiers, police, informers, or spies. On one particular occasion, I did ask him if he had been a member of any 'Hit Squad'.

Without answering me directly, he told me that he had been walking into town one evening and that at the Bandon Road and Barrack Street junction, he recognised some volunteers (not of 'H' Company) coming up Barrack Street with a man in custody who was well known to him. On inquiring what was going on, he was told that following brigade orders, they were taking him, Denis 'Din Din' Donovan, a suspected spy, to be executed, but first, they were taking a detour to the Lough church as he had wished to receive his last confession.

John Joe offered to accompany them, but they declined, advising him to continue on his way to town as they knew both men were acquaintances. Donovan's body was later found the following day in Ballygarvan. I never again asked him about his involvement in 'Din Din's' or any other execution, knowing it was something he did not wish to talk about or discuss. On reflection I now realise you can't ask someone you admire and love if they killed anybody as it implies they have.

# State Side

It was in 1927, a few years after the Free State was established that John Joe, together with his friend and fellow volunteer Jerry O'Brien, decided to travel to the USA.

On arrival, he settled in New York. This was a journey many other volunteers, particularly on the anti-Treaty side, decided to take. He had every intention of staying there permanently as he enjoyed the city and had found acceptable work there. He met up with his old comrade Conn Neenan, who had also travelled to the States. John Joe found employment with the Brooklyn Edison Company Inc. New York. Conn meanwhile got involved in the Irish Sweepstakes and Waterford Glass.

The sweepstakes, while illegal in the US, were a very successful fund-raiser with tickets being sold via the network of Old IRA volunteers. The funds then made their way back to Ireland by innovative routes avoiding any custom checks.

As a single, good-looking young man, John Joe enjoyed the freedom of New York, attending many social and sporting events with his relations and friends. It seemed that he was finally free of the responsibility of protecting old comrades and safeguarding himself from his enemies.

John Joe and Jerry O'Brien on the way to New York

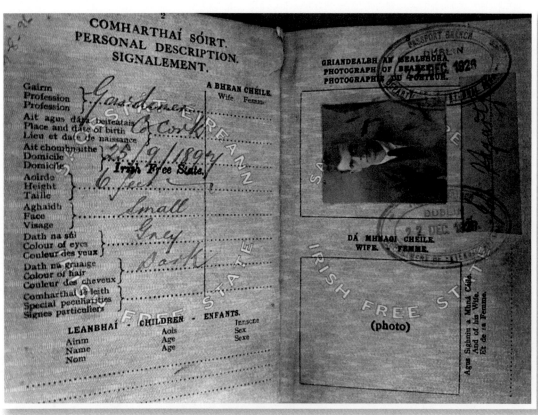

John Joe's passport

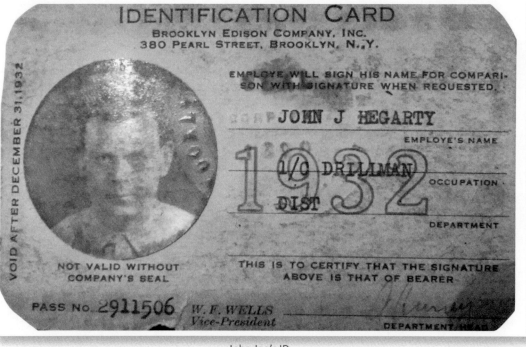

John Joe's ID

Brooklyn Edison Co head office 1920s

# John Joe Returns to Cork

However, in the early thirties, his father asked him to return to Ireland in order to take over the running of the market gardens business. He felt honour-bound to comply with his father's wishes as he was grateful to both his parents for risking their own lives by making 'The Laurels' available to him, his sisters, and their comrades during both wars.

This request was unusual as he was not the eldest son. It was the custom of the time that when land was being passed from one generation to another, it should go to the eldest son.

# St Finbarr's National Hurling & Football Club

Once back in Cork, both he and Conn Neenan revitalised their passion for the GAA and St Finbarr's club in particular. In fact, it was John Joe who sourced and arranged the acquisition of the land for the club with the help of the Mannings who were close family friends, while Conn provided the financial support. Our Auntie Greta (Manning) was a member of that family.

The grounds and pitches at the end of Mannings' Lane was later named Neenan Park and were officially opened by Conn in the early sixties. The opening day included a senior hurling match between the Barr's and a New York selection. The New York team included the great Peter Doolan who remained in Cork after the game and helped both the Barr's win the 1965 County Championship and Cork win the 1966 All Ireland. Conn had arranged with John Joe that his son Jack would run the sideline (always a Barr's ball ) for the senior game. Meanwhile Jim was picked to play in the curtain-raiser representing the Lough Street Leagues versus a North City selection. The event attracted a few thousand in attendance including John Joe and other members of the Hegarty family. In 1970 a state-of-the-art clubhouse was built by the far-sighted committee of the time.

Official opening of Clubhouse 1970

# Pouladuff and Bishopstown Coursing Club

In November 1933, John Joe attended the AGM of the Pouladuff and Bishopstown Coursing Club and was elected onto its committee as the assistant field Marshal. The club was established in December 1929 while he was in New York. He remained a member of the club for the remainder of his life and involved all the family during the coursing season.

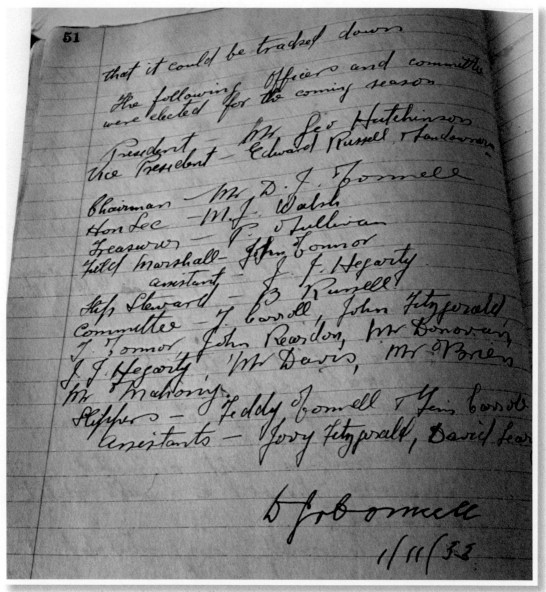

John Joe joining Pouladuff & Bishopstown Coursing Club on his return home

# Meeting Liz Allen

Liz Allen

He met my mother, Elizabeth Allen (Liz), who was born on the 28th of February 1908. She had established a dressmaking business on the Bandon Road and was best friends with Nan, who was still residing at 'The Laurels'. It was she who made the introductions. John Joe had arrived back home with dollars in his pocket and a Crombie coat that needed alterations.

In 1934, Nan married John James Fennell, whose family were general merchants from Kyrl's Quay. She eventually left the Laurels to reside in Inniscarra, where she later established a shopkeeping business. They had a family of two sons, John and Gus.

# Patrick Allen

Liz's father, Patrick Allen, like so many Irishmen, served in the British army with the Royal Artillery, fighting during the First World War for the freedom of small nations. He was a blacksmith by trade and a 'horse whisperer' by profession. He was not a qualified vet, but he had a great reputation for treating injured horses. Horses had played a vital role in transport and the moving of heavy artillery during the First World War. During 1915 his war records show his theatre of war was mainly in France.

Ireland was a very important provider of horses to Britain for decades and crucial to the British Army at this time. He would write home to his son John Robert, in Belgooly, encouraging him to work hard at their forge business until he returned from war. As all post was censored, he used a coded message urging John Robert not to volunteer and join the British Army.

Patrick Allen

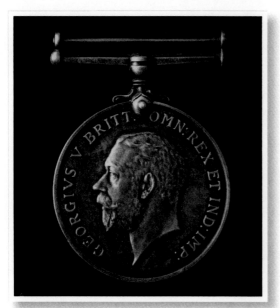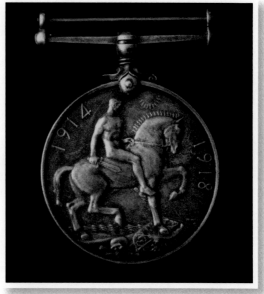

Patrick Allen medal

# David Allen

Meanwhile, Liz's uncle David Allen had come from Kinsale to live in Togher in a house built adjoining the Sarsfield's lands. David was a personal friend of Michael Collins. He had been appointed and served as a Sinn Féin magistrate during the War of Independence. When the Civil War was over, he became an early Free State Peace Commissioner. He stood unsuccessfully for Fine Gael in the 1948 general election.

David Allen canvassing 1948

▲▼ General Election: 4 February 1948

## ◀▶ Cork Borough
Cork Area *(Munster)*

| 5 Seats | | 16 Candidates | | | | | | | |
|---|---|---|---|---|---|---|---|---|---|
| Electorate: *not available* | | | | | | | Quota: 7,480 | | |

| First Preference Votes | Count Details | Transfer Analysis | Party Details | Biographies | Other Information | | | | |
|---|---|---|---|---|---|---|---|---|---|
| **Candidate** | **Party** | **1st Pref** | **Share** | **Quota** | **Count** | **Status** | **Seat** | | |
| David Allen | FG | 911 | 2.03% | 0.12 | 0 | | | | |
| Richard Anthony | Lab | 2,688 | 5.99% | 0.36 | 0 | | | | |
| Stephen Barrett | FG | 1,496 | 3.33% | 0.20 | 0 | | | | |
| Seán Casey | Lab | 987 | 2.20% | 0.13 | 0 | | | | |
| John Fennessy | CnaP | 1,423 | 3.17% | 0.19 | 0 | | | | |
| Walter Furlong | FF | 3,601 | 8.02% | 0.48 | 0 | | | | |
| James Hickey[1] | IND | 4,507 | 10.04% | 0.60 | 0 | | 5 | | |
| Jack Lynch[1] | FF | 5,594 | 12.47% | 0.75 | 0 | | 2 | | |
| Seán MacCarthy | FF | 2,747 | 6.12% | 0.37 | 0 | | | | |
| Dr Patrick McCartan[1] | CnaP | 2,346 | 5.23% | 0.31 | 0 | | | | |
| Pa McGrath | FF | 5,092 | 11.35% | 0.68 | 0 | | 3 | | |
| Seán O Dubhghaill | IND | 260 | 0.58% | 0.03 | 0 | | | | |
| Dr Tom O'Higgins[1] Snr | FG | 7,351 | 16.38% | 0.98 | 0 | | 1 | | |
| Michael Sheehan[2] | FG | 409 | 0.91% | 0.05 | 0 | | | | |
| Michael Sheehan[1] | IND | 4,898 | 10.91% | 0.65 | 0 | | 4 | | |
| Liam Stack | CnaP | 565 | 1.26% | 0.08 | 0 | | | | |
| Total poll | | 44,875 | | | | | | | |

Election Results 1948

# 1948 General Election

During this election, John Joe canvassed for his old IRA comrades Pa McGrath and Martin Corry and all other Fianna Fáil candidates contesting the Cork constituencies. This was also the election that resulted in Jack Lynch first becoming a TD. The election itself caused embarrassment to Lynch as his election was achieved with the help of the Glen Rovers hurling club, members of whom ran an independent campaign to have him elected. This despite the objections of the other Fianna Fáil candidates, as well as Lynch himself as he was an admirer of McGrath and others.

A compromise was reached when Tom Crofts negotiated with the club so that they would also canvas for the other Fianna Fáil candidates. Years later, in 1966, Martin Corry was one of a group of Munster TDs who persuaded Lynch to become the compromise candidate for Taoiseach

As a result of the election, John A. Costello was appointed Taoiseach of the first inter-party government, despite not being the leader of his own party. His

leader, Richard Mulcahy, was not acceptable to some other ministers, such as anti-Treaty man Sean McBride, due to his role and activities during the Civil War.

Costello had no involvement in either the War Of Independence or Civil War and was acceptable as the compromise Taoiseach.

During his first term, Costello introduced the Republic Of Ireland Act (1948), resulting in Ireland withdrawing from the British Commonwealth of Nations. Meanwhile, Mulcahy served as Minister for Education in his cabinet.

# Married Life of John Joe & Liz

John Joe and Liz

When they married on the 1st of June at the Lough chapel, John Joe asked Denis (Dee) Forde, his nephew (Mamie's son), to be his bestman, while Liz asked her sister Eileen to be her bridesmaid. Dee married Catherine (Kitty) Twomey from Killowney, Old Head, Kinsale in 1961. Her father Daniel was arrested in 1921, under the Restoration of Order in Ireland Act 1920 (ROIR), for his involvement in the struggle for independence. He was sentenced to six months imprisonment with hard labour, spending time in Spike Island internment compound. (One hundred years later their son John was a member of both the Spike Island and Fort Camden Meagher redevelopment committee. Liz's great grandnephew Adam Duggan was part of the team that restored all the artillery and vehicles that are now on display as part of the tourist attraction.) Eileen, who never married, was at that time living with her widowed uncle David Allen and his children in Doughcloyne, Togher. Eileen and her sister Maud would in later years establish a shop on Shandon Street known as 'Miss Allen's,' to which John Joe would deliver vegetables and fruit regularly, as well as to other shops, especially Molly Owen's (a sister-in-law of Mary O'Leary).

The Owens family were a very strong republican family, and it was not unusual for Molly and her friends to light bonfires in Blackpool to welcome President de Valera whenever he visited Cork. The President would never fail to stop and have a chat with her over tea or coffee.

He and Liz subsequently had a family of eight children, namely, Elizabeth (Betty), Anne, Pauline, Patrick (who passed away as a baby), Edward, Eileen, Jack, and Jim. Apart from Betty and Anne, who were born in a nursing home on the northside of the city, Pauline and the rest of the children were born at 'The Laurels,' under the medical care of Nan's brother-in-law, Dr. Denis Fennell.

After their wedding, they made 'The Laurels' their home. It is said that his father Patrick, by then a widower living in the house, was very proud of Liz and would drive her everywhere in the pony and trap. The first time he returned from the markets, he handed her the money and said, 'you are now the woman of the house and as such in charge of the finances'. John Joe continued with this practice for all his married life.

Both Liz and John Joe were very warm people, both as parents and friends. I, the youngest, was born into a very loving and hard-working family. Seeing both parents up close every day working from home and always around, I realised from an early age that their only objective was to see that their children did not want for anything - this they did in abundance. They were both self-employed working from home, and as soon as any of their children were in a position to lend a hand in either the gardens or shop, they volunteered our services with no demarcation. They instilled in us a very strong work-ethic, which all of us carried forward for the rest of our lives.

It was also a tribute to their hospitality and good nature that all our relations made sure to call and or stay in the house whenever they were in Cork, regardless of whether they came from England, New Zealand, USA, or closer to home, places like Dublin, Cobh, Belgooly, Kinsale, Clare or Cork city. Some of our relatives, especially aunts and uncles, came to our home to recuperate when they were ill.

## Military Prison in the Field

### SPIKE ISLAND
CORK HARBOUR

### Records of Republican Prisoner
### 1921

# Daniel Twomey

Killowney, Old Head, Co. Cork
Age: 28
Occupation: Farmer
6th Division arrest No.: 17 I.B. 969B

While he was in the Spike prison compound, he was served
with an Internment Order before his release date. Instead
of being released, he was further detained as an internee.

He was transferred to Spike Island internment compound
on 14 November 1921.

He was transferred from Spike to Maryborough (Portlaoise)
Prison on the night of 18/19 November and released from
there on 8 December 1921.

T. F. Kennedy, Major,

Commandant, Military Prison in the Field

## Military Internment Compound

### SPIKE ISLAND
#### CORK HARBOUR

Records of Republican Internee
1921

# Daniel Twomey

Killowney, Old Head, Co. Cork
Age: 28
Occupation: Farmer
6th Division arrest No.: 17 I.B. 969B

While he was in the Spike prison compound, he was served with an Internment Order before his release date. Instead of being released, he was further detained as an internee.

He was transferred to Spike Island internment compound on 14 November 1921.

He was transferred from Spike to Maryborough (Portlaoise) Prison on the night of 18/19 November and released from there on 8 December 1921.

Internees were arrested by Crown Forces and imprisoned without trial, for their suspected involvement in Republican activities during the Irish War of Independence

T. F. Kennedy, Major,
Commandant, Military Prison in the Field

Hegarty Family 1960s. John Joe, Eileen, Edward, Betty, Anne, Jack, Pauline Jim and Liz

Hegarty Family 1990s. Edward, Gus Fennell, Eileen, Anne, Jack, Betty, Pauline and Jim

# Old IRA Pension

In 1935 John Joe applied for and was subsequently awarded an old IRA pension under the terms of the Military Service Pensions Act, 1934 (ref 34 SP/11081). It's worth noting that one's life had to be in danger in order to receive this pension. Both Nan (ref 60594) and Mamie (ref 60389) were also granted pensions for their service to the state during the specified time.

However, for whatever reason, they both waited until the mid-forties to apply for their pensions. Many other members of Cumann na mBan never applied for their pension for various reasons, one being not to embarrass their husbands, who may not have been actively involved during the War of Independence

My grandfather Patrick Hegarty, who gave his permission and approval for the use of 'The Laurels' and his grounds as a bomb dump and safe House for the brigade during the War of Independence and Civil War, an unsung hero in his own right, died on the 31st of October 1938.

'The Laurels' land and life insurance policies were subsequently legally transferred to John Joe's sole ownership following his demise.

M.S.P. 34/4.

# AWARD CERTIFICATE.

| Any further communications on this subject should be addressed to ~~the~~ and the above number quoted. | ROINN COSANTA, (Department of Defence), GEATA NA PAIRCE, (Parkgate), BAILE ÁTHA CLIATH (Dublin). |
|---|---|

...............20 January, ........19..37.

I am directed to inform you that in accordance "with the terms of the Military

Service Pensions Act, 1934, the Minister for Defence has granted you a pension of

£.7..15..7.. (Seven Pounds, Fifteen Shillings per annum, which is payable as
and Seven Pence)

from the 1st October, 1934, and which will be subject to deduction under Section

20 (1) of the Act in respect of receipts by you from Public Moneys.

I have also to state that it is your duty to inform the Minister at once of any

receipts by you of any Public Moneys as defined by Section 20 (1) of the Act.

*J. J. Horgan*
t/c Rúnaí.

* To..Mr. John Joseph Hegarty,...............

.....The Laurels, Pouladuff Road,........

...........Cork.

MD.

**Section 20 (1) of the Mil. Ser. Pensions Act, 1934, defines Public Moneys as**—" Any remuneration, pension, or allowance payable out of public moneys, whether provided by the Oireachtas or out of the Central Fund or by means of the poor rate or any other rate imposed by a local authority."
**Extract from Mil. Ser. Pensions Act, 1934, Section 19 (1)** & **(2)**—" If any person with a view to obtaining either for himself or any other person a grant or payment of a pension under this Act makes, signs, or uses any declaration, application or other written statement knowing the same to be false, such person shall be guilty of an offence under this section, and shall be liable, on summary conviction thereof, to a fine not exceeding twenty-five pounds, or to imprisonment for a period not exceeding six months, or at the discretion of the Court to both such fine and imprisonment.
If any person so convicted as aforesaid is in receipt of a pension obtained by reason of such false declaration, application, or other written statement he shall forfeit such pension as from the date of such conviction."

N.B.—This Certificate is no security whatever for debt. It should be carefully preserved, as it will be of the greatest assistance to you when completing the Pension Warrants, which will be sent to you.

* In the event of the death of the person to whom this Form is addressed, the person who notifies the death to the local Registrar of Deaths should deliver this Form and any other Pension papers held by deceased, to him, and will receive from him the sum of one shilling for so doing.

[1866]  L.6606—Wt.8502—Dem.8721—Gp. 28—11/34—20,000—Hɛʟʏ's Lᴛᴅ.

Certificate of Pension

# Liz & the Shop

Liz came from a family business background and, as a result, had a general grocer shop built at the side of the house. She had a very holistic but also a commercial approach to business and to life in general, an approach which she nurtured and filtered down to her children.

There was one occasion, however, when a customer called to the shop to pay for the week's papers that I had delivered in Earlwood estate. She handed over sixpence, and Liz was about to hand back three pence when she was told that covered the delivery charge. When I came home from school, John Joe informed me that my mother wanted to see me. I knew I was in trouble (again) but had no idea why! In a serious voice, she questioned me about the 'delivery charge', inquiring as to how long it had been going on for. When I replied 'forever in the new private estates', while looking to a smiling John Joe for support, she said that the money should go to the shop. However, as no support was forthcoming, she knew she was on a loser, so we compromised and agreed to split the difference. My father and mother worked as a perfect team without ever speaking a harsh word.

Shop at the Laurels

# Customer Care

Liz, always aware of her customers' financial position and sensitive to their needs, never demanded cash immediately for essential purchases, instead opting to offer them credit if they so desired. She managed this by keeping a record of their purchases in a credit book. People at this time did not have a lot of money, so a little went a long way.

She always treated people fairly in her dealings but did not suffer fools easily. I can remember when a young priest, new to the parish, visited the shop one day and asked if he could put some turkeys in the fridge as he had been given a few as presents for Christmas. She told him in no uncertain terms that he did not need all of them; she would put one in the fridge for him, but she would find a deserving home for the rest. Her customers were always allowed to use the shop fridge whenever they needed to freeze any of their goods, mainly fish.

The shop telephone also operated as an extended community service. Having the phone, which was a rarity at the time, also, of course, brought custom to the shop. Many's the time emergency calls for neighbours came in the middle of the night and were dealt with immediately by a member of the family.

No longer solely dependent on markets, my parents' business began to thrive. The sale of vegetables and poultry had always been their mainstay in the shop, but in a short time, they expanded the business, becoming newsagents as well as tobacconists and oil merchants. This was a time when there was a huge expansion of house building in Cork and particularly around the Pouladuff area, surrounding parishes and townlands. Many families were moved from the city centre, some out of lanes and tenements known as the 'Marsh', to the suburbs. While this was great for these families, it was also the beginning of the end for the market gardens of the areas.

# Christmas Tree Tales

While John Joe was an expert at market gardening, unlike Liz, shopkeeping was not his forte. There was one particular Christmas period when a lady came into the yard and asked to see the Christmas trees. He held up one out of a hundred and said, 'this is the pick of the crop for ten shillings'. She asked if he had one another like it for seven shillings and sixpence. He told her to go into the shop and finish the rest of her shopping, and he would sort her out by the time she got back. He got me to hand him the saw saying, 'son, watch and learn'. He took about a foot off the tree and stuck the end in the ground. On her return, he proudly showed her the 'new' tree, costing seven and six. However, she said she preferred the ten-shilling one! I did not hang around for his reaction.

Every Christmas, we delivered trees to the customers we knew could not afford them and left them in their gardens under darkness, so no one was any the wiser.

# Health and Safety

Many of the shop practices would not pass today's health and safety regulations, such as cutting meat just after filling a can of paraffin oil, wrapping fresh bread in an old newspaper - which allowed the customer to read the news, old as it was while eating the bread when he or she got home! Or selling loose cigarettes and matches. None of these practices ever killed anyone, but it did get physical when occasionally, a few young, smart asses would call into the shop on a regular basis and ask if my mother kept dripping. On informing them that we did, in fact, sell it, while making a fast exit out of the shop they would invariably shout out, 'put a bucket under her'. That was my cue to leap the counter and plant a few slaps around their ears and elsewhere. They were gluttons for punishment.

# Friday, Fish Day

It was a family tradition to eat only fish on a Friday as the Catholic Church had instructed its members to abstain from meat as an act of discipline. It fell to John Joe to collect the fish from Anne's husband, Haulie O'Driscoll, in Clayton Loves. He religiously delivered it to Anne's home first in Turner's Cross before going to 'The Laurels,' and from there to his other children's homes, Jack's and Carmel's in Glasheen, Edward's and Mary O's, Pauline's and Barry O'Regan's in Summerstown, and finally to Eileen's and Con O'Sullivan's in Bishopstown. This also gave him time to see his young grandchildren, whom he adored.

# Open House

Our home became an open house, and you were never sure about whom you were going to meet or sit down with at mealtime. Visitors ranged from commercial travellers calling to the shop, workers from the garden, family or relations, and of course guards dropping in for a meal and a smoke while on the beat. With all the traffic at mealtime and the kettle on the boil all day, I am sure there was not much profit made in the shop

Marie Marks from New York, a relation of John Joe and Nan, pictured at The Laurels 1960s
with Pauline, Nan and Gus Fennell, Betty, Liz and John Joe

by the end of the day. People continually called to have a chat and ask John Joe for advice, so much so that he was affectionately known as the Lord Mayor Of Pouladuff.

There was one occasion when the guards were patrolling in their new and probably first squad car, when they decided to drop in for their habitual cup of tea; afterwards, they took me for a spin back to their barracks in Togher. When we got there, they locked me up in a cell for fun. One of the guards, known for his dark sense of humour, quipped, 'bet his old man would not burn it down now'. It was years later that I came to really understand what he was referring to.

# West Cork Railway

I distinctly remember a one-off trip on the West Cork railways with John Joe when he brought me to see the Barr's play Beara in a senior football championship match. (Eileen's husband Con [Paddy] O'Sullivan being the star of the Beara team.)

I remember thinking that while he had many dangerous adventures on these and other railway tracks, my only claim to fame regarding same was with some friends placing a halfpenny on the tracks in the hope that a passing train might flatten it, enabling me to pass it off to an unsuspecting shopkeeper as a penny. We never targeted Hegarty's shop. In any event, one could never accuse my mother of being an unsuspecting shopkeeper. She'd have nailed us on the spot, and that would have ended that particular activity. All of this just changed within one family generation

# World War Two or 'The Emergency'

Like many of his comrades, both pro and anti-Treaty, John Joe was actively involved in national service between the years 1939 and 1946, during the Second World War. Ireland remained neutral during this conflict (although biased towards the Allies), and it was referred to officially as 'The Emergency'.

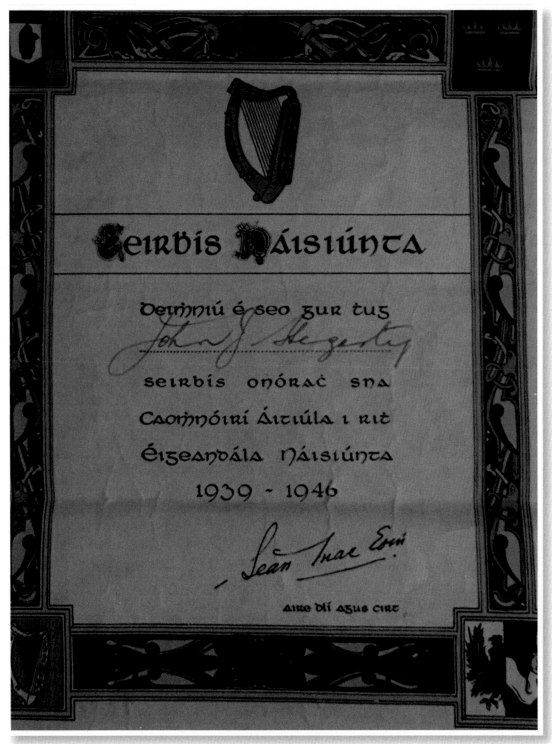

Seirbís Náisiúnta

Deimniú é seo gur tug

*John J. Hegarty*

seirbís onórac sna

Caomhóirí Áitiúla i rit

Éigeandála Náisiúnta

1939 - 1946

*Seán Mac Eoin*

Aire Dlí agus Cirt

John Joe Service Certificate

# Awarding of Service Medals

In May 1942, the Minister of Defence, Mr. Oscar Traynor TD, himself a veteran of the War of Independence, was granted government approval to issue a service medal for those Volunteers and Cumann Na mBan members who served their country during the War of Independence, 1917-1921. These were to be issued to those with a military certificate which enabled them to receive the pension under the 1934 Act.

The medal with the inscribed bar has the words 'Comrac', meaning combat or struggle, and was only awarded to people who played an active part in military operations against the British Crown forces. The colour of the ribbon is black and tan, which was an unusual choice as these colours were a reminder of one of the most hated corps troops ever deployed by the British in Ireland. The period between 1919 and 1921 is sometimes referred to as the 'Tan War' because the soldiers wore a mixture of army khaki and RIC navy blue uniforms. Up to the late sixties, there were only 15 166 'Comrac' bar medals issued, while 47,613 without a bar were awarded. However, some are still being awarded posthumously. One of the most recent 'Comrac' medals was awarded to the family of Joe Murphy in 2019. This was achieved when his grandniece Shirley Kelleher, with the support of her local TD Donnchadh Laoghaire ( a Barr's man), made strong representations to the government.

The medal was presented at a ceremony in Cork City Hall, with Mick Finn (another Barr's man!) as Lord Mayor. I am proud to say John Joe, Mamie and Nan were all awarded the 'Comrac' medal.

Medals

# Hand Over of Medal

Up until the early 1970s, we had a dry dump in the gardens, which consisted of garden spoils, and particularly horse manure, delivered by the Cork Corporation, as there were many stables in the surrounding areas. There was also buried treasure like glass bottles mixed in with the rubbish. The spoils were good fertiliser for the land, and I could claim money back on the bottles, so, all in all, great recycling was in evidence before we knew what it meant.

When I was about five or six, I broke some bottles as I was bringing them down to the shop. The next day I fell from one of the apple trees and seriously cut my knee on the broken glass. There was blood everywhere; it was touch and go, and I was terrified I'd have to have my leg amputated. Fortunately, I avoided that fate and ended up getting several stitches under the supervision of Dr. Christy Sullivan, our family doctor. I was confined to bed and not allowed to move my leg for weeks. One day John Joe came and sat at the side of the bed and pinned his medal on my top, saying, 'all brave soldiers should have a medal, and you are our brave soldier'. It is still one of my treasured possessions.

On reflection, one item no longer in my possession is an old unloaded handgun that I found while exploring the stables. Finding artefacts of this kind wasn't completely unheard of. We often stumbled upon Sam Brown belts in the different sheds, and we once found an old British Army helmet in the yard, which John Joe used to feed Tom the Horse oats. (Tom was treated like royalty by John Joe, as he was not only a workhorse but an invaluable means of transport when goods were being delivered to shops and markets.) On showing my discovery to John Joe, he said 'leave it to me'. It's the last I ever saw of it.

John Joe and Liz continued working the gardens and shop while raising their family in the most loving environment possible, making sacrifices so their children could enjoy their lives. This was no mean feat - looking after seven active children.

Despite the gardens and the shop being places of work, they also provided us with a playground and a place of enjoyment. Apart from giving us an insight into business, they gave us the freedom to explore nature and inculcated in us a love of animals.

# Old IRA Men's Association

On his return from the US, John Joe became very involved with the Old IRA Men's Association, which had been established in Cork in 1934. Some of the founding members were Tom Crofts, Florrie O'Donoghue, and Liam Deasy, men who were very familiar with all the Hegarty family and the brigade's activity at 'The Laurels'.

Membership was open to those who served in the Irish Volunteers, Irish Republican Army, and Fianna Eireann from 1914 to 1924, and also their supporters. The majority of members appear to have been current or former anti-Treaty supporters and may have had associations with Fianna Fáil, which was in power in the 1930s. Their aims included working for the achievement of an Irish Republic and defending the rights of those who suffered because of national service. They also supported Irish business, language and sports.

The association and its members were deeply involved in providing colour parties for commemorative events, including the handing over of Cork Jail, where many of their comrades were tortured and executed, to University College Cork. They also provided guards of honour for deceased members. The earliest one I have recorded for John Joe with other members of the association was for the funeral of Patrick J. Murphy, Ballygarvan of 'F' Company, when his remains were returned to Cork from New York in 1949, for burial in Douglas Cemetery. Murphy was given a full military funeral.

On the 22nd of June 1956, a very prominent member died, and John Joe had the privilege of leading the guard of honour at the funeral of his friend and former comrade Pa McGrath T.D., Lord Mayor of Cork, through the streets of the city. This was one of the biggest funerals ever seen in Cork as McGrath had been a very popular public figure. The corporation councillors were led by McGrath's brother-in-law, A.A.(Gus) Healy

Leading the funeral cortege of Lord Mayor Patrick McGrath (credit Cork Examiner)

# Joe Murphy's House

In 1960, John Joe was a very active participant in the organising committee and colour party when with his old surviving comrades from 'H' Company 2nd

Battalion 1st Cork Brigade erected a plaque to the memory of Joe Murphy at his family home on the Pouladuff Road.

Also in attendance were men such as Sean O'Hegarty, Tom Barry, Florrie O'Donoghue, and Michael Murphy. This was a very proud day for the Murphy family, with all of the Hegarty family also present. It was also a proud day for us to see our father John Joe, normally a quiet, unassuming, gentle giant of a man, who spoke so little about his experiences, on parade with his surviving comrades. It was this event also that first gave me an interest in the history of that period.

Other commemorations honouring Joe happened in 1926 when Fianna Fáil, which had just been established, named one of their first cumanns after Joe. In later years Sinn Fein followed suit for their south city cumann. The Cork Corporation also honoured Joe Murphy by naming a road in Ballyphehane after the martyr when it was being developed in the 1950s and 1960s. 'The Boy from Pouladuff' produced by his grandniece Shirley Kelleher and 'My Unsung Hero,' written and produced by Maurice Dineen to mark his centenary, are now available on YouTube.

Unveiling of plaque at Joe Murphy's house (credit Cork Examiner)

# Phairs Cross

Similar to the honouring of Joe Murphy by survivors of 'H' Company, a plaque was unveiled at Phairs Cross, by Conn Neenan of 'G' Company, to acknowledge its role as its headquarters (it was also the workplace of intelligence officer Jeremiah Keating) in the struggle for independence. As a mark of respect, it's also the tradition of St Finbarr's hurling and football teams to pass the site on their way to the club as county champions.

All Cork Brigade companies would support and attend these special occasions.

Con Neenan and Jeremiah Keating at the official unveiling 1960. Credit Cork Examiner

# New Memorial at Republican Plot 1963

A few years later, I can remember meetings being held at 'The Laurels,' where the plans and drawings for a new memorial to be erected at the republican plot in St. Finbarr's Cemetery were discussed. Funds were raised from many sources, and a sum had also been bequeathed by J. J. Walsh, former TD, and minister, on his demise.

This was to be unveiled on St.Patrick's day in March 1963. John Joe was very proud to be one of the organisers of this event, as many of his fallen comrades were buried there. Sean O'Hegarty was the chairman of the organising committee, but due to illness, unfortunately, he could not attend the unveiling.

An attempt was made by the 'New' IRA to blow up the monument, which could have resulted in John Joe's death and that of many of his Old IRA comrades. This could also have included the President, Eamon de Valera, who had travelled to Cork to officially unveil the monument. The question of whether this was an assassination attempt on the president's life or just a symbolic destruction of the monument is open to debate.

Other invited guests on the main platform included Terence MacSwiney's daughter Maire, her husband Rory Brugha (son of Cathal Brugha), and their son Cathal MacSwiney Brugha. Members of the Hegarty, Fennell, and Forde families were also in attendance.

The bomb was timed to explode at 3.15. Whether it was a.m. or p.m. is moot. The general consensus is that it was detonated early in the morning as the men were planting and checking the device. Years later, when I discussed the incident with members of the de Valera family, they were unaware of any assassination attempt on the president's life.

Of the two people responsible for the explosion, one, Desmond Swanton, was killed, and the other, Gerry Madden, was seriously injured. Madden, under a garda escort, was treated in hospital. Initially, the authorities did not know what organisation was responsible for the atrocity, and they requested the assistance of the surgeon, Mr. John Barrett, who cooperated and they solved their problem. He did this by establishing what type of metal was embedded in his leg. When he was told by Madden that it was a Jacob's tin box, the guards immediately knew it was the 'New IRA.' Unfortunately, his leg had to be amputated, and he also had an eye removed by a Dr. Madden (no relation).

Dr. Barrett issued his invoice to the IRA office, and it was honoured. However, when Dr.Madden issued his invoice sometime later, it was rejected, as word came back that the men had no authority to carry out this operation, that they were, in fact, on a solo run. Their actions led to a lot of divisiveness among Cork republicans. There is a file on this event in the hands of the Cork Gardai, but the file is empty!

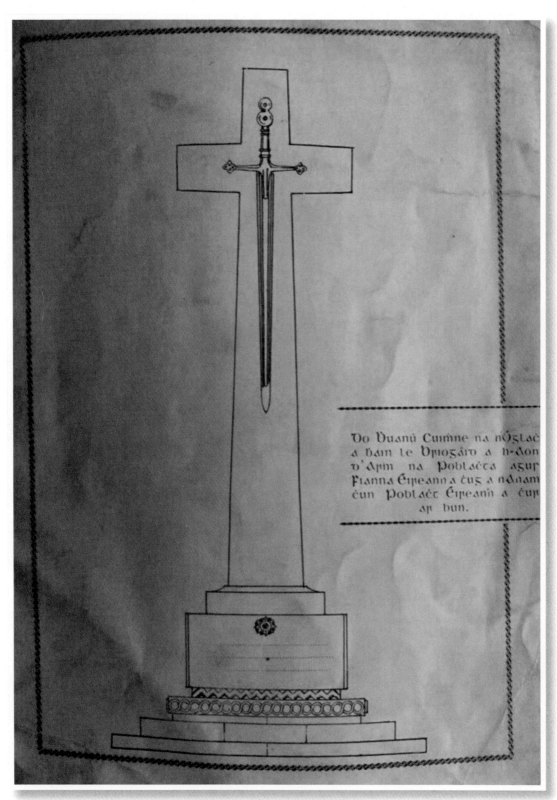

Programme Republican Plot 1963

# The Memorial.

HE twenty-five feet high memorial, which is the work of Seamus Murphy, R.H.A., is made of limestone. The base, twelve feet by eight feet, is a simple block with a carved recessed member having the following inscription cut on it:

Do Buanú Cuimne na nÓglaċ
a bain le Dniozáid a h-aon
d'Anm na Poblaċta agur
Fianna Éineann a tuz a nanam
ċun Poblaċt Éineann a ċun
an bun.

The Cross is plain with a well proportioned diminish on front and sides. The arms also taper out, and the effect is graceful and dignified against the background. Carved in high relief on the cross is an enlarged replica of a famous sixteenth century Irish sword which was found in the river Barrow near Monasterevin, Co. Kildare, in 1935 and is now in the National Museum. The design thus combines the sword as a symbol of valour and the cross as a symbol of sacrifice.

The Memorial has been erected by a Committee representing all the Battalions of Cork No. 1 Brigade. The Committee was formed in December, 1960, under the Chairmanship of Sean O'Hegarty. The fund raised for the purpose has been contributed to mainly by the surviving members of the Bridge, both in Ireland and abroad, with a notable and substantial contribution from those now residing in the United States of America.

A number of Memorials had already been erected in other places in the Brigade area, such as that in what was formerly the yard of Cork Jail but is now part of University College grounds, and where the bodies of men executed at Cork military barracks were buried.

Some of the Battalions have commemorated their own dead with memorials such as those at Midleton, Dripsey and Macroom. Sites of other engagements and deaths have been marked, as at Ballycannon, Dublin Hill and elsewhere, but it has long been felt that the Republican Plot at St. Finnbar's cemetery, which contains the largest number of Brigade dead and which has such a prominent and public location, should be marked with a worthy memorial which would embrace all the one hundred and fourteen men whose names appear on the Brigade Roll of Honour.

There are sixty graves in the Plot, including three of members of Fianna Eireann and three of members of Cork No. 3 Brigade. Some graves are unmarked, and on these the Memorial Committee will erect headstones.

# Easter Lily

From that date on, I can never remember an Easter Lily being openly displayed in the house. For many years John Joe felt the republican plot had been desecrated by the 'New IRA'. However, it did not prevent him from attending official ceremonies organised by the Old IRA Association or personal private visits to the plot to honour his former comrades.

# IRA Split

The 1960s saw the words of Brendan Behan, author and staunch republican, come true when he suggested that the first item on any republican agenda is the split. There were so many organisations claiming to be the true successors of the men and women of 1916. This even impacted on the wearing of the Easter Lily, which was originally created by Cumann na mBan to honour such people. After the split in official Sinn Fein/IRA in 1969/1970 and the emergence of Provisional Sinn Fein/IRA, the Official IRA wore the Easter Lily with an adhesive, and the Provisionals wore it with a pin. This resulted in one side being called the 'stickies' and the other 'pinheads'.

John Joe and Liz held strong constitutional republican views and always discouraged us from joining or supporting any of the new organisations in the early seventies. The boys all joined the 3rd Cork Cubs and Scout (off Summerhill North), and the girls were members of the Guides and different charity organisations.

One other event took place at the republican plot when another burial took place without permission and in defiance of Cork Corporation's wishes. John Joe and his Old IRA comrades were again saddened and annoyed this time because it was only a short time since the site was attacked, and now there was an attempt to hijack the plot. The funeral passed a short distance from 'The Laurels' at the Pouladuff and Pearse Road junction with a heavy garda presence. I can remember the tension with a large crowd and the tricolour very much in view.

There was sympathy for the family for their loss, but also anger at the organisers who had ordered shots to be fired over his house.

# Easter Ceremonies and Grave Visits

It was traditional for John Joe to attend the Cork Easter ceremonies with members of the family, beginning with Betty, Anne, and Pauline together with the families of his old comrades. A photo of him attending Thomas Kent's grave at Collins Barracks appeared in the Evening Echo - it was taken in the early 1970s. Also in attendance is his nephew Denis Forde PC, son of Mamie, and Fr. Gerard Keohane, the army chaplain of the time and a former teacher of mine in Farranferris, presided over the ceremony.

This tradition has been continued by family members when attending ceremonies and grave visits nationwide.

Easter ceremonies at the grave of Thomas Kent at Collins Barrac in the 1970s.

Credit Cork Examiner

Easter Ceremony Collins Barracks 1966. Photo includes Mamie, Mrs E Kelleher and Mrs W Furlong. John Joe and Nan and family members would also have attended this ceremony. Credit Cork Examiner.

Pauline and Frank O'Regan with
Anne O'Driscoll
at Hegarty Family Plot

Anne's husband Haulie and his son
Pat with Taoiseach Garrett
Fitzgerald and General Tom Barry

Jim and Senator Gerry Horkan at Unveiling at
Cabinteely Park 2016

Gus Fennell at Crossbarry c 2020

Mamie at Crossbarry 1960s

# Joe Murphy Commemorations

The fiftieth anniversary of Joe Murphy's death was commemorated and organised by John Joe and his former comrades at the republican plot in October 1970. It was a small gathering of family and friends with pipers from the Cork Volunteers in attendance. An oration on Joe's life and times was delivered by Gerry Carroll, a local chemist on Barrack Street and a member of the Cork Corporation. Gerry held strong republican views and became a member of the short-lived political party Aontacht Eireann (Irish Unity).

This party was established by Kevin Boland in 1971 when he refused to support Jack Lynch as Taoiseach; Lynch having sacked Charles Haughy TD and Neil Blaney TD as a result of the arms crisis. They had all been ministers in a Fianna Fáil government.

On the centenary of his death in October 2020, a ceremony was arranged by The Togher and Ballyphehane Centenary Committee at the republican plot, but due to the Covid 19 Pandemic the attendance was confined to a small number. The Hegartys were represented by both Eileen and Jack, who continued the family tradition. After the laying of a wreath by Joe's grandniece Shirley Kelleher, the lone piper (our cousin) Adam Duggan played the lament 'Dawning of the Day', also known as 'Raglan Road'.

Jack and Eileen O'Sullivan

Yvonne Hegarty and her children
Jack Joseph and Cliona Culloty

# Hegarty Politics & Sport

Keeping the family interest in politics alive, John Joe and the family were very active in the 1965 and 1969 general elections, when Paddy Forde, son of Mamie, was a candidate. We had the privilege of seeing Paddy elected to the Dáil in the 1969 general election as a Fianna Fáil TD for the Mid-Cork constituency. It was during this same general election that Martin Corry resigned as a TD. Paddy died in 1972 after only a few short years in office. In the subsequent by-election Gene Fitzgerald of Fianna Fail was elected. In later years, Fitzgerald became a government minister, including Minister for Finance.

The Hegartys, to a man and woman, always showed a keen interest in sport, and each of them participated with some degree of success. John Joe's love for his greyhounds encouraged us to go coursing and attending the race track. Betty, Anne, Pauline and Eileen played Camogie with St. Als. Edward played with the Barr's, Sully's Quay and Farna, before leaving the GAA behind to play soccer with Crofton Celtic alongside his brother-in-law Barry O'Regan. Jack joined the Barr's and later Bishopstown GAA, representing Cork at an under-age level, and is an active member of Bandon Golf Club. Jim played competitive hurling and football with Ballyphehane teams such as Joe Murphy's and Joseph Plunkett's, and later St Finbarr's. He represented Cork and Limerick Insurances in soccer. Later in Dublin, he played with the civil service hurling and football club and became captain of Grange Golf Club.

When it came to Munster championship time, we travelled with John Joe to the finals. The early 1960s were barren times for Cork, with Tipperary and Kerry dominating. The breakthrough came in 1966 when Cork won both Munster finals, and the hurlers won the All Ireland, with a Barr's man, Gerald McCarthy, as captain. Con (Paddy) O'Sullivan, Eileen's husband, had finally won his first senior football Munster medal. He repeated it in 1967 but unfortunately lost the All Ireland final to Meath. Between 1968 and 1969, I had the good fortune to win a county medal with the Barr's, and Harty Cup and All Ireland medals with Farranferris, with John Joe and family members in attendance. There was always great excitement at 'The Laurels' whenever a cup or trophy was brought home. John Joe and Liz always encouraged the family to enjoy playing and supporting all sports.

Cork Lord Mayor Mick Finn visits Jim at Grange Golf Club
on Captain's Charity Day

**PADDY FORDE**

PADDY FORDE, of Fivemilebridge, Ballygarvan, comes from a family that were prominent
in the struggle for Independence and has been con-
nected with Fianna Fail since his youth.

A publican and garage
owner, he was elected to the Cork County
Council in 1967 and has won recognition as
an outstanding public representative. He is a
prominent member of many subsidiary com-
mittees of the County Council, such as the
Rehabilitation Committee, the South Infirmary
Committee and the Library Committee. He is
also a member of the Cork Health Authority.

There is every reason to believe that he
would make an outstanding Dail deputy who
would at all times be at the service of his
constituents. He is worthy of your full confidence.

# VOTE FOR THE
# Fianna Fail
# Candidates

1, 2 and 3 in the order of your
choice.

Paddy Forde

# Well known family

THREE members of a well known South East Cork family are shown in the picture above along with DEPUTY GENE FITZGERALD, second from left.

They are TEDDY, DENIS and HILARY FORDE, who were attending the annual dinner dance at Cork Airport held by the Paddy Forde Fianna Fail Cumann.

The Cumann is named in memory of their brother who was a Deputy for Mid-Cork.

The Forde family originally came from Ballinhassig.

Teddy, who is a vintner, now resides at Ringaskiddy, Co. Cork, while Hilary, who is a builder, lives in Gould Street, Cork, as does Denis who carries on the family undertaking business at South Gate Bridge.

Their brother, Paddy, died in May 1972 and his seat for Mid-Cork went to Gene Fitzgerald in the by-election.

*George Brown*

Credit Cork Examiner.

# 1973 Freedom Of The City

In March 1973, John Joe was honoured to be one of the invited guests of the Cork Corporation at the conferring of the Freedom of the City on Eamon de Valera, President of Ireland, at the Concert Hall City Hall Cork.

There was always a picture or bust of de Valera in the house, as well as the Proclamation and photos of Lord Mayors Mac Curtain and MacSwiney, so this gave him immense pleasure to be invited.

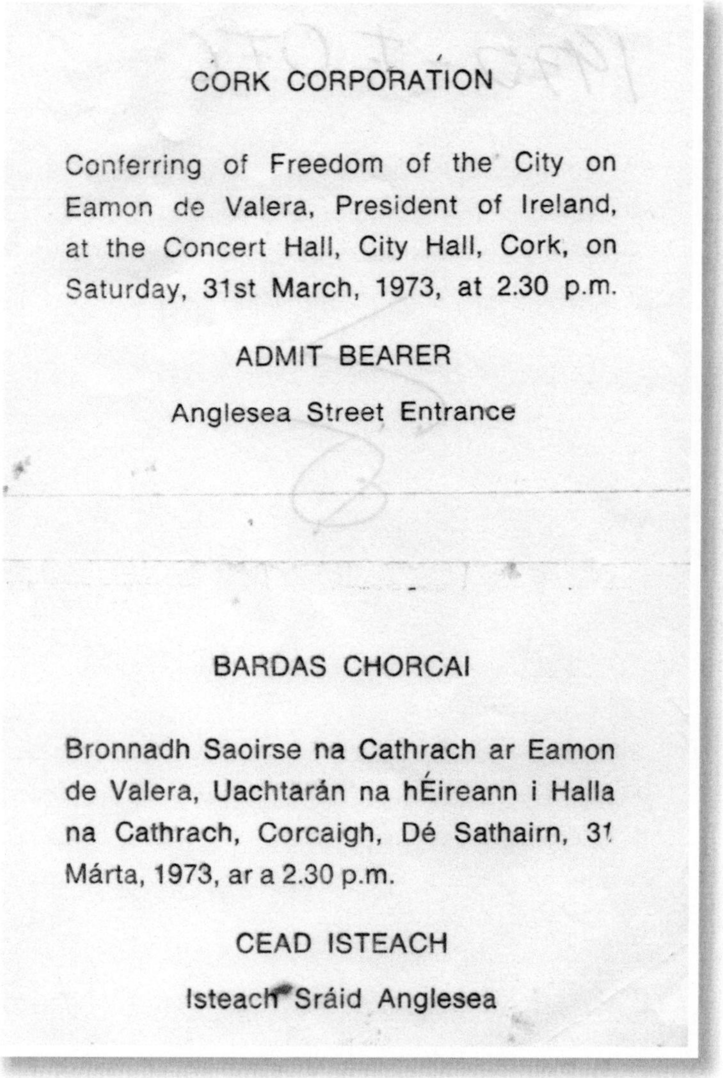

CORK CORPORATION

Conferring of Freedom of the City on Eamon de Valera, President of Ireland, at the Concert Hall, City Hall, Cork, on Saturday, 31st March, 1973, at 2.30 p.m.

ADMIT BEARER

Anglesea Street Entrance

BARDAS CHORCAI

Bronnadh Saoirse na Cathrach ar Eamon de Valera, Uachtarán na hÉireann i Halla na Cathrach, Corcaigh, Dé Sathairn, 31 Márta, 1973, ar a 2.30 p.m.

CEAD ISTEACH

Isteach Sráid Anglesea

**CORK CORPORATION**
**CITY HALL**
**CORK**

**BÁRDAS CHORCAÍ**

**HALLA NA CATHRACH**

**CORCAIGH**

28th March, 1973.

A Chara,

Freedom of City - President de Valera.

I enclose admission ticket to special meeting of the Corporation and informal reception at the City Hall on Saturday 31st March next.

You are specially requested to be in your place at the Concert Hall not later than 2.30 p.m.

Admission will be by the Anglesea Street entrance.

The procedure at the Special Meeting of the Corporation will be as follows:

1. Roll call of Members.

2. The Lord Mayor will recite opening prayer, all present standing.

3. The City Manager will read resolution conferring the Freedom of the City of Cork on the President.

4. Speech by the Lord Mayor.

5. The Lord Mayor will call on the President to affix his signature to roll of Freemen of Cork City and will present to him a casket containing scroll.

6. Reply by the President.

7. The Lord Mayor will declare the Special Meeting at an end.

8. The national anthem will be played.

9. The Lord Mayor, President and party and members of the Corporation will leave the Concert Hall by the door to the west of platform.

Mise, le meas,

PATRICK CLAYTON

# John Joe's Funeral

While continuing to work the gardens, which were now reduced in size, as a large portion had previously been sold off in the 1960s for housing development, John Joe became suddenly ill and passed away on the 6th of June 1973.

I can remember a procession of men calling who were anxious to see him before he died. He was given a full military funeral, similar to Mamie's in 1967 and Nan's in 1971. All are laid to rest in their family graves in close proximity at St Joseph's Cemetery. All the arrangements were organised by his nephew Denis Forde and his family undertakers.

My last memory of him before the lid was placed on top of the coffin was as he was leaving the house, my mother kissing his forehead. Outside the house, a large crowd had gathered to pay their final respects. There was a similarly large crowd when we arrived at the church that evening and at the funeral the following morning. They were saying goodbye to a man who had never been an elected politician but who had always been there for those who sought his advice or help.

When the service at the Lough church was over, and as we travelled to the cemetery, we came to a temporary stop at the Pearse Road and Pouladuff Road crossroads, at which the guards were on duty. This was a very poignant moment as they stood to attention and saluted as the hearse carrying the coffin passed. The coffin was draped in the tricolour, a flag which he had fought so hard to protect. On arriving at the cemetery, we were met by a large crowd of people, family and friends who had gathered with many of his old comrades in their trademark hats. They, together with an Army contingent from Collins Barracks, performed a guard of honour. Under their commanding officer, they fired a volley of shots over the grave at the conclusion of the religious service. There was also a large representation from the greyhound industry.

# Death of well-known greyhound enthusiast

The death occurred unexpectedly last week at his residence, The Laurels, Pouladuff Road, Cork, of Mr. John Joe Hegarty, a founder member of the Cork Co. Open Coursing Clubs' Association, on the committee of which he represented the Pouladuff and Bishopstown Coursing Club. He had a lifelong connection with greyhound sports and had reached the age of 76 years but was still a man of vigorous health. A man both big in character and stature he will be missed by his old and young friends in both branches of greyhound sport.

There was a very large gathering of Cork and County coursing and track personnel at removal of the remains, including Mr. James M. Lantry, hon. treasurer of the Irish Coursing Club, and chairman of the Cork Coursing Club; Mr. Con Murphy, Bord na gCon; Mr. Noel Holland, manager, Cork Track and Mr. Pat Murphy, hon. sec. Cork Coursing Club.

One of the most notable greyhounds bred by Mr. Hegarty was Urhan Bridge which at one time held the 550 yard record at Youghal.

Obituary

Death Notice

# Meeting of Cork Corporation

It was very much appreciated by all the family that at the Cork Corporation meeting, which was held at City Hall on the 11ᵗʰ of June 1973, a vote of sympathy was passed and communicated to his widow, Elizabeth Hegarty of Pouladuff Road.

The vote was proposed by Comhairleor Healy (AA Healy TD, North East Ward). John Joe had always supported Gus Healy at election time and was a personal friend of long-standing. Gus was a brother-in-law of former Lord Mayor Pat McGrath TD.

---

**From:** Timmy O'Connor [mailto:timmy_oconnor@corkcity.ie]
**Sent:** 30 July 2015 13:16
**To:** Jim Hegarty <Jim@hegarty.ie>
**Subject:** Minutes 1973

Dear Mr Hegarty,

Further to your call of yesterday, i have checked Council minutes for the meetings of 11 June and 25 June 1973. Both meetings concluded with votes of sympathy, with 'members standing in silence', but no minute's silence as such is recorded. At the meeting of 11 June, one of the votes of sympathy was for Mrs Elizabeth Hegarty, Pouladuff Road, on the death of her husband. Other votes concerned J Morgan, P O'Sullivan, Thomas Egan, Rev MT Blakley (11 Jun) and Mr and Mrs T Lynch, Mrs Lucey, and M Scally (25 Jun).

The papers you have regarding interments in the Republican plot sound very interesting, and I and my colleague Brian McGee, chief archivist, would be very glad to discuss these with you at some point.

Best Regards,

Timmy

---

Timmy O Connor, Local Government Archivist
Cork City & County Archives
Seamus Murphy Building
33a Great William O'Brien Street
Blackpool, Cork
Tel. : +353 (0)21 4505 876
Fax +353 (0)21 4505 887
Web: www.corkarchives.ie <http://www.corkarchives.ie/>

Find us on Facebook: http://facebook.com/corkarchives/

# Final Resting Place

All three Siblings are buried at St Joseph's Cemetery in their family plots:

Hegarty grave is section 1 St Joseph's Row 1, Plot 31;

Fennell grave is section St Michael's Row 1, Plot 10;

Forde grave is section St James' Row 1, Plot 37.

Jim wearing chain of office

Jack wearing chain of office

## HEGARTY

THE family of the late Elizabeth Hegarty, St. Anthonys 5 Mercier Park, Curragh Road (late of Pouladuff Road) wish to thank most sincerely all those who sympathised with them in their recent bereavement; those who attended the removal, Rosary and funeral; those who sent Mass cards, letters of sympathy and floral tributes; and to those who travelled long distances. A special word of thanks to all the clergy and Dr. Christy O'Sullivan, Grand Parade, who were so kind and attentive; to the very kind neighbours and friends who helped so much and in so many ways. As it would be impossible to thank each one individually, we trust this will be accepted by all, and assure you always of our heartfelt thanks and gratitude. The Holy Sacrifice of the Mass has been offered for all your intentions

Liz Death Notice

# The Laurels Sold

Members of the family continued to live at 'The Laurels' until it was sold by Liz in 1977. However, prior to its sale, the remaining gardens were sold to Mamie's son, Hilary, who developed the site and constructed six houses on the land. All the works were carried out by his family firm, with the exception of the electrical work, which was carried out by Jack Hegarty Electrical Ltd., Liz's son's firm. Jerry O'Brien, whose grandfather Jerry served as an officer in 'H' Company and who had travelled to the US with John Joe, worked on-site for Jack. Jack himself devoted a lot of his time to the Irish Electrical Contractors Association for the benefit of its members. Recognised as a stalwart organiser, he was encouraged to play an executive role in the Association. He subsequently served as its National President for a number of years. Jim also became President of the National Brokers' Association in 1987. Jim and Jack were the first Corkonians to be elected to these respective positions.

Liz and her daughter Betty went to live in Mercier Park, where her daughter Anne resided until she passed away on the 31st of October 1987. Her church service was at Turner's Cross Church, which again was attended by large numbers of family and friends but also by large numbers of her old customers from her shop in Pouladuff.

She had a reputation for always looking after customers, especially those with large families who were in need of support. It was not unusual that many of the food items purchased in the shop without payment were recorded in the 'book'. It must also be said that after the shop was closed, many came to her to settle their debts.

Both parents left a family legacy to cherish.

LOCAL GOVERNMENT (PLANNING AND DEVELOPMENT) ACT, 1963

## NOTIFICATION OF A GRANT OF

## OUTLINE PERMISSION / ~~PERMISSION / APPROVAL~~

under Section 26 of the Act.

To : ...Mrs...Hegarty.,..............................

.c/o.Aston.Deller.&.Morgan,.............  Reg. No. T.P...6673...............

.13,.South.Mall,..........................

.Cork................................  Application
Received : ..24th.January,.1977.........

APPLICATION BY ...Mrs..Hegarty,.c/o.Aston.Deller.&.Morgan,........................

OF .13,.South.Mall,.Cork...............................

FOR :—

OUTLINE
~~OUTLINE PERMISSION~~ / PERMISSION / ~~APPROVAL~~

FOR.....Residential.development...............................

AT ..."The.Laurels".,.Pouladuff.Road.......................

Further to notification of decision to grant dated....23/3/1977...........................

the Cork Corporation hereby conveys a grant of

## OUTLINE PERMISSION / ~~PERMISSION / APPROVAL~~

for the development/~~retention~~ described subject to the conditions (if any) set out in the said

notification.

The permission/approval is also subject to further approval being obtained in accordance

with article 5 of the Local Government (Planning and Development) Act, 1963, (Permission)

Regulations, 1964, prior to the

| | the development |
| commencement of | any part of the development other than |
| | ......................... |
| | ......................... |

# Dublin

When I moved house in Dublin, one of my immediate neighbours was Marie MacSwiney Brugha, daughter of Terence MacSwiney and daughter-in-law of Cathal Brugha. I shared many stories about Cork with her and produced for her a MacSwiney Cup medal won with the Barr's. When she passed away, I had the privilege of being part of her guard of honour at our parish church at St.Teresa's, Mount Merrion Dublin.

Another neighbour of mine was Dr. Richard Mulcahy, son of Dick Mulcahy, the man responsible for ordering the execution of many of the anti-Treaty prisoners during the Civil War. Dr. Richard was a great storyteller, a renowned cardiologist, anti-smoking advocate, and a thorough gentleman.

Remarkably, when in 1917 Terence MacSwiney married Muriel Murphy (Muriel was a member of the Murphy distilling family) in Bromyard Herefordshire, England, his best man was none other than Richard Mulcahy. Mulcahy would go on to become Commander in Chief of the National Army after Michael Collins was killed in 1922.

Pro and anti-Treaty families are all reconciled and living in harmony. I am privileged to say I received a signed copy of both of their books - *History's Daughter*[6] and *My Father The General*[7].

My immediate neighbour Blanaid Quinlan (nee McAuliff), originally from Friars Walk, is a granddaughter of Jeremiah Keating, an intelligence officer in 'G' Company based at Phairs Cross, a friend and fellow comrade of John Joe, Nan, and Mamie. I often visited the shop, his place of work with John Joe, never realising the strong connection between the two and the secret past they shared.

While they were protecting one another's families, 100 years later, Blanaid was doing the very same for my family when our grandson was rushed to ICU in Holles Street Maternity Hospital, where she took wonderful care of him. Just a case of history repeating itself.

---

6    ISBN:0-86278-948-6
7    ISBN-13978-1905483953

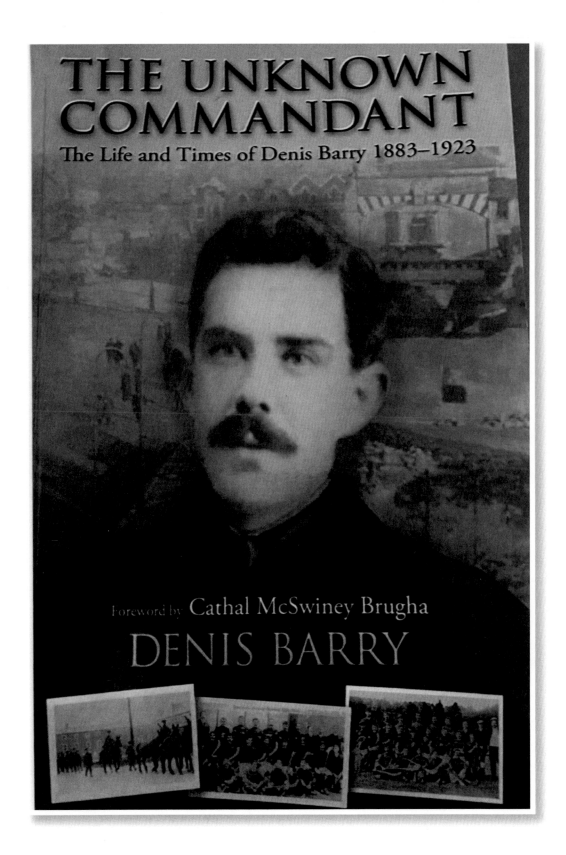

# THE UNKNOWN COMMANDANT

## The Life and Times of Denis Barry 1883–1923

Foreword by Cathal McSwiney Brugha

## DENIS BARRY

# Denis Barry - The Unknown Commandant

In his book *The Unknown Commandant: The Life and Times of Denis Barry 1883-1923*[8] published in 2010, the author, Denis Barry's nephew, also Denis Barry, devotes a chapter and gives a very comprehensive account of the unveiling of the republican plot in 1963. In it, he mentions John Joe Hegarty as part of the organising committee.

Another chapter in which he addresses the role of Cumann na mBan is headed: A Tribute to Brave Women. He states that Cumann na mBan held its first meeting in Wynn's Hotel, Dublin, in April 1914. By the middle of 1920, the women were fully organised in Cork, with the Hegarty clan to the fore in helping the volunteers in all their activities. Denis mentions his mother-in-law, Mary Ellen Hegarty (nee Moore) a sister of Sean O' Mordha, who was secretary of Cork Comhairle of Sinn Féin at that time.

Mary Ellen was a relation of the Hegarty family known to us as Aunt Sis. She, Mamie and Nan all served together in the different branches. Mary Ellen coincidently married Mick Hegarty (no relation to us), and they lived on College Road. Aunt Sis's other brother Dan Moore was a teacher in the North Monastery, and with Jack Lynch and Dr. Saunders he was a founder member of St. Anne's Adoption Society.

When part of our market gardens were sold for development in the 1960s, Boston Park was extended into them. Denis and his wife Patsy bought one of the houses and set up their home there. He used to give me grinds in Irish for the Leaving Certificate; money well spent! As the land had been cultivated for well over a century, the soil was very fine and as black as soot, a challenge for any development. This resulted in a court case involving some new householders and the developer.

8    ISBN-13:9781848890299

# Remembering Commandant Denis Barry

In his native village of Ballymartle, the Fianna Fáil cumann is named after Commandant Denis Barry. Two of Mamie's sons, former chairman of the Cumann, Teddy Forde, and his brother Paddy, a TD, were very much involved in promoting the annual commemorations which highlighted his life and deeds. They, together with others, were also responsible for erecting a monument in his honour, which was opened in 1966 by Martin Corry TD. The bridge in the village of Riverstick is also dedicated in his honour.

# Unfinished Business! Ranks to be Reinstated

There is one more chapter of the period yet to be completed in our story, that of restoring the ranks of volunteers and officers that took the anti-Treaty side during the Civil War.

In October 1922, at the height of the Civil War, Piaras Beaslai, Communications Director for the Free State, issued a number of directives, including that henceforth the anti-Treaty side were now to be referred to as Irregulars and were not 'Republicans,' 'IRA,' 'Forces' or 'Troops,' nor were the ranks of their officers to be disclosed.

This order was never rescinded, but now 100 years later, hopefully, this can be revisited, resulting in all anti-Treaty Volunteers and their officers being reinstated as ranking Irish soldiers and officers that were involved in the struggle for a free and independent Ireland.

It is not right in my view that these brave men and women who fought for their country's independence went to their graves without this being rectified.

- Directives are sent to the press by Free State director of communications, Piaras Béaslaí to the effect that; Free State troops are to be referred to as the "National Army", the "Irish Army", or just "troops". The Anti-Treaty side are to be called "Irregulars" and are not to be referred to as "Republicans", "IRA", "forces", or "troops", nor are the ranks of their officers allowed to be given. No letters about the treatment of Anti-Treaty prisoners are to be published. The words "attacked, commandeered and arrested" as used to describe their actions are to be replaced by, "fired at, seized and kidnapped".

Béaslaí Directive

# 1916 Medal

In 2016, to commemorate the 1916 Easter Rising, I was presented with medals from Fianna Fáil by Eamonn O'Cuiv, grandson of Eamonn de Valera, and Cathal MacSwiney Brugha, grandson of Terence MacSwiney and Cathal Brugha, in recognition of John Joe's role in the struggle for freedom.

This was a very proud occasion, particularly when Cathal spoke so passionately and linked John Joe, Mamie and Nan to his grandfather's Terence MacSwiney's activities in Cork. I also had the privilege of being invited to Glasnevin Cemetery as an official guest to commemorate the centenary of the Easter Rising by David Bunworth, Chairman of Glasnevin Trust.

1916 Family medals presented to Jim by Cathal MacSwiney Brugha

1916 Family medals with Éamon Ó Cuív

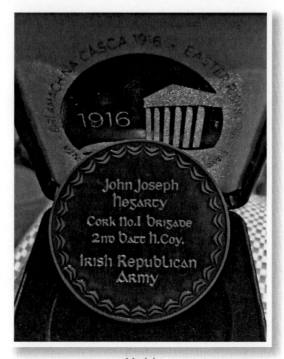

Medal

# Acknowledgements

I'm grateful to so many people. Dr. Yvonne Crotty (DCU) who, on reading the first draft, encouraged me to include vignettes and anecdotes and, above all, not to skim the surface but to drill down in the research. Well, the drill-head is now in the repair shop! John Joseph Hegarty for his invaluable research and photographs. The Forde and Fennell branches of the family for all their very positive input and support. Seamus Leahy for sharing with me so much of his in-depth knowledge and photographs of the period.The Irish Examiner,Cork Public Museum and Michael Collins for the use of their photography. Cathal MacSwiney Brugha for his kind words and support. Tadhg Quill-Manley for the gift of his family's book *The Man With The Long Hair*. Ger O'Kelly for the use of his red pen when I foolishly thought I had finished. Billy O'Brien and the Togher Historical Association for helping to bring this story to a wide audience at an early stage. Donal Murray for his advice and support in bringing the story to the publishing stage. Jeremy Murphy of JM Editing & Literary Agency for his expert advice and copy-editing. All the staff at Hegarty Financial Management Ltd.  Roddy Ahern,Mick Bracken, Tom Crotty, Una Crowe, Kieran Crowley, Maurice Dineen, Conor Dwan, Mick Finn, Margaret Hanratty, Fergal Hanvey, Niamh Hassett, Brian Hurley, Shirley Kelleher, David Moran, Eoin Pol O'Callaghan, Kieran O'Connell, Lisa O'Sullivan, Ged Walsh.

To my wife Maura, daughters Louise and Niamh Hegarty, their spouses Ross Craigie and Aidan Ryan for your patience, kindness, love and support.  With special mention to Ava, Rhys, Lauren and Aaron.  To my brothers and sisters for sharing our wonderful journey together.

I hope my story will encourage or inspire you to enjoy researching and documenting your family story.

# About the Author

Jim Hegarty was born at home in 'The Laurels' on the Pouladuff Road. He is a keen sportsman and has spent most of his working life in the financial services industry. Having spent a decade working for an insurance company, he established his own financial brokerage. In 1987, he became National President of the Brokers' Association. He was appointed a Peace Commissioner in 2000. He has served as a director of both private and public companies.

Jim Hegarty

# To Be Continued

Family Photo Maura and Jim, Louise, Ava, Aaron, Rhys, Lauren and Niamh

The Hegarty Clan 2019

# Abbreviations

AGM - Annual General Meeting

ASU - Active Service Unit

Barr's - St Finbarr's Hurling and Football Club

DCU - Dublin City University

Dev - de Valera

GAA - Gaelic Athletic Association

ICU - Intensive Care Unit

IRA -Irish Republican Army

John Joe - John Joseph Hegarty

Liz - Elizabeth Hegarty

Mamie - Mary Francis Forde (nee Hegarty)

Nan - Joanna Fennell (nee Hegarty)

PC - Peace Commissioner

RIC - Royal Irish Constabulary

St. Als - Saint Aloysius

Taedy -Timothy Owens

TD. - Elected Member of the Dáil

# Appendices

Patrick (Paddy) Moran. 1916 - 1993 was born in Clogheen, Co Tipperary. In 1940 he, along with many young men, joined the Irish Army to serve in what later became known as " The Emergency ".

He was most fortunate in being posted to the Intelligence Marine & Air Corps section based in Dublin Castle. There he served under Colonel Dan Bryan O.C. Bryan had two great interests, namely improving the education status of his young charges and the intelligence gathering achievements and brilliance of Michael Collins during the war of independence. Bryan took his principles and practices in intelligence gathering from the Michael Collins way - simplicity and at all costs avoid detection.

Learning the craft of intelligence gathering from Colonel Dan Bryan, Paddy Moran in later years delighted in relating the logic and story of Michael Collins's superb strategy of successfully being able to regularly gather, in a safe location, here in Dublin a small group of Volunteer Officers for briefing purposes. Collins knew that Matches and Masses were much too easy to infiltrate, so therefore, were of no benefit in the guarantee of avoiding detection.

Instead he, along with the assistance of a sympathetic hospital worker at the Rotunda Hospital( and more importantly without the knowledge or suspicion of the Hospital authorities), used the scheduled visiting times as cover to have his
men discreetly enter the Hospital. His men just joined and blended in with the
Visiting Dad's attending at visiting times, armed with a bunch of flowers - how appropriate. These active service Officers would then discreetly adjourn to a small basement area and secretly and securely conduct their briefing sessions
in full confidence of concealment. Later at the end of visiting times they would leave the Hospital, mingling with all the other Dad's, catch their Bus or Train
and safely return home to their Provincial bases. In all the times Michael Collins operated this clandestine operation, the authorities failed to uncover this simple and effective reporting protocol.

There is a direct personal link to Colonel Dan Bryan O.C Intelligence Corps and Michael Collins. It is well documented that Dan Bryan in the early years joined the Volunteers from U.C.D Medical School and actively served in a Collin's unit
- thus he personally knew Michael Collins from the start.

David. T. Moran
Kilternan. Dublin
April 2020

1

Letter from David Moran. PG 38 Intelligence Work.

CONSTITUTION.

Cumann na mBan is an independent body of Irishwomen, pledged to work for the establishment of an Irish Republic, by organising and training the women of Ireland to take their places by the side of those who are working and fighting for a Free Ireland.

Name ........................

Address ........................

irishstamps.ie    Clúdach Chéad Lae | First Day Cover

POST

## Centenary of the founding of Cumann na mBan

On April 3, 2014, An Post issued a stamp to commemorate the centenary of the founding of Cumann na mBan on April 2, 1914 in Wynn's Hotel, Dublin.

Cumann na mBan (The Irishwomen's Council) was a women's nationalist organisation founded to 'advance the cause of Irish liberty'. Its constitution provided for the use of force by arms against the Crown Forces in Ireland. Founding members included Jennie Wyse Power, Agnes O'Farrelly, Louise Gavan Duffy and Agnes MacNeill.

Their patriotic aims attracted thousands of Irish women eager to play their part in the fight for Irish independence. By October 1914, Cumann na mBan had upwards of 60 branches, some having dozens of members.

In 1916, Cumann na mBan members played a key role in the Easter Rising, although their roles were mainly non-combatant. After the Rising and with many of the key revolutionary leaders dead or imprisoned, strong support for the work of Cumann na mBan ensured the struggle for independence continued.

The stamp and first day cover were designed by Ger Garland. The stamp features Cumann na mBan members driving at the head of the funeral of citizens shot during the Howth arms landing (courtesy of Kilmainham Gaol Museum). The first day cover features the membership booklet of Cumann na mBan member, Sighle Humphreys (courtesy of UCD Archives and Mrs. Cróine Magan).

An Post 100th Anniversary commemorative stamp. First Day of Issue - 2014. PG 50 Nan goes full time with Cumann Na mBan.

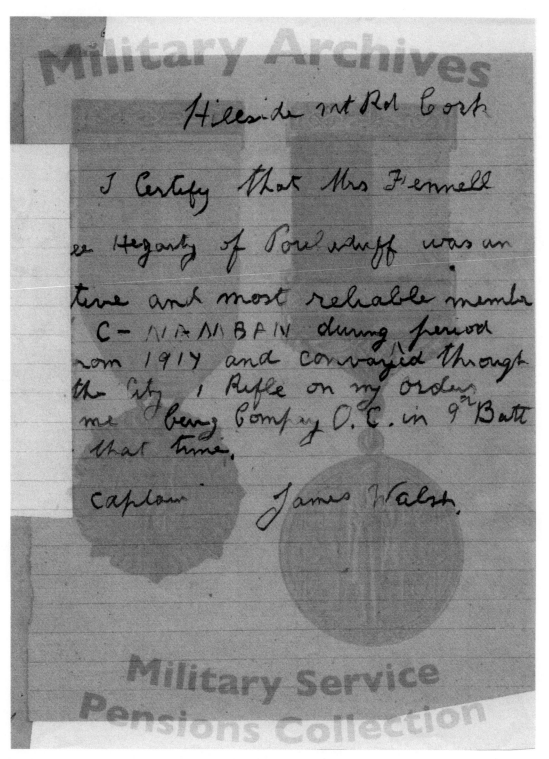

Hillside mt Rd Cork

I Certify that Mrs Fennell
ee Hegarty of Poulnduff was an
tive and most reliable member
C — NA MBAN during period
rom 1917 and conveyed through
the City 1 Rifle on my orders
me being Compy O. C. in 9ᵗʰ Batt
that time.

Caplain        James Walsh.

Walsh's Letter of support. PG 50 Nan goes full time with Cumann na mBan.

For the Board of Service Pensions
From Personl Knowledge of this Ladys activities in Cumn na mBan I can bear witnes to the valve her servies during my period of O/c Cork I Brigade

Sean Hegart

Cork 14/5/45

Letter of support from Sean Hegarty. PG 50 Nan goes full time with Cuman na mBan.

### EVIDENCE OF APPLICANT (SWORN) 23rd August, 1945.

1. Joined C. na mBan in 1916 and a member up to and during Civil War.

6. My brother had a small dump but I had nothing to do with it.   There
were always men coming and going to our house.   I took stuff, parcels,
to Tipperary twice.   I got a rifle in Miss Herlihy's shop in 1919, and
carried it through the city.     Jack Meagher stayed with us.    I carried
guns around Cork for Seán Mitchell about 3 times.    I took 4 revolvers
from Greenmount for Elizabeth Fort attack.    Our house was ideal for
safety.    Only myself and my brother were at home then.    Fellows would
come and leave me stuff and I'd put it away temporarily until my brother
would come.    Nobody used stay in the house regularly - only on odd
occasions.    No wounded or sick men in the house.    Carried despatches
into the City 15 or 20 times.    Our place was used by S. Hegarty.    I was
i/c. of stuff for the Togher Bks. burning.

Truce:   No attendance on Camps.

Civil War:   I went with stuff to Crossbarry and just escaped a raid by
the military.    Men called to the house and some stayed casually.

In the Civil War we were raided by the military; whole house searched
and they took away a motor cycle.

### EVIDENCE OF MRS. MITCHELL (SWORN) 24th August, 1945.

6. Mrs. Fennell came in the spring of 1921 and stayed one night when our
house was a dump.    She came often in the day-time.

7. In May 1921 she took two of my children when the Brigade staff was in
my house.

9. She came to the Col. once with me.

### EVIDENCE OF SEÁN HEGARTY (SWORN) 24th August, 1945.

6. In December 1920 I wanted a house during the day.   I worked there during
the day and went in to the city in the evening to H.Q.   Messages were
coming during the day; she fed me also; she was very discreet; I was
there for a month.    I've no knowledge of her afterwards.    It was the
Battn. O/C. got the use of the house for me.

--------------------------------------------------------------------------

### EVIDENCE OF SEÁN MITCHELL          24th January, 1946.

6. She was in Pouladuff in the Tan War.    I knew it was a much used house.
Even though her brother was on the run, other men stayed there.    We
used dump a bit of stuff in the market-garden.    She brought stuff, a
gun and 2 rounds, out of my house (Clarke's Bridge) to Pouladuff.    She
could have carried guns 3 times for me.

7. It was the only house in the district that was any good.

9. During the Civil War I used her to contact people in Cork and bring me
out some stuff.    She also carried stuff to Crossbarry.    I was there at
Xmas 1922.

Military record of Nan. PG 50 Nan goes full time with Cuman na mBan.

The Refixes

Application of Mrs Mary F Forde
Kaisers Bill
Bassach St Cork

I am aware that Mrs Forde ( nee Hegarty)
was a very active mumber of the Cumn na
mban in Cork City

During years of 1917 to 1918
she was very active in argouizing functions
to Raise funds for the Volunteers. Her house
in Pouladuff (outskirts of the City) was very
extencively used for Coummuaction with the
9th Batt. area. Herself ond sister handled very
many despatches. Her house was very Constantly
used by the Brigade oge Sean Hegarty in
Company with other Officers

In 1920 she was a
Constant Visitor with Comforts to I.R.A.

Prisoners and also housed men on the Run including Meagher Molloy and others from Tippeary & Limerick. She conavied Ammunition on sebeard occasions from her husbands store who [strikethrough] Procuard it from U.S Soldiers & Sailors at Coabh She was Constantly bring this ammunition from Cobh to Cork. (Her Husband was working at Cobh)

She Procured a Rifel the Property of an ex [strikethrough] British Saldier in Blarney She discourrood it in his house had it conived to Cork City

Towards the end of the Tan Period she Married and then resided in Greenmount also in the suberbs. She Contunied [strikethrough] to carry Ammunition.

I have no hesitation in saying that Mrs Ford Cleam is an outstanding and I would be very Pleased to give evidence behalf.

To Tom Croft

Letter of support from Tom Crofts. PG 78 A touch of Blarney.

Ref. No. 60389.                          Mrs. Mary Forde.

## EVIDENCE OF APPLICANT (SWORN) 23rd August, 1945.

1. Acknowledged signature to and contents of claim form.

2. A member of Lehenagh Branch from Oct. 1916. Collections, parcels for prisoners. I was President of the Branch of 20 or 30. Mary
3. Richardson got a pension. Routine.

4. I brought some guns (a parcel) from Cobh to Cork that I got from my husband the time the Yanks were there. Started branches of C. na mBan in 4 districts.

I got a gun from D. Hegarty and I brought it to my husband in March 1921. I brought ammunition from Cobh about 4 times to Peter St. from my husband (parcels about 9 lbs.). Visited men in jail. Jack Maher and Molloy were kept in the house; others who were released also came; 3 or 4 men would be kept in the house at a time for a month; this was done right up to the Truce; a dozen or more would come for dinner or tea; it was all done at my own expense. I carried ammunition 3 or 4 times from Greenmount to Pouladuff. I didn't carry parcels of ammunition 10 times before the Truce, about 10 times in all. Arms were kept in the house and I was responsible for them while they were out.

TRUCE: I organised the C. na mBan for the Upnor. I brought despatches from Ballygarvan to Lehenagh, about half a dozen times and an odd message from D. Hegarty to my husband. The catering in the house started in 1918; then I had the local Capt. Seán Hegarty used hold Brigade meetings frequently in the house. Located a rifle and ammunition in a pub and told her husband who took it away (5th March 1920). The carrying of ammunition from Cobh took place during and after the Yanks left Cobh; No one knew of it only my husband.

CIVIL WAR: 6 men were brought in by my husband about the time of the Passage landing; 2 of them were "bloody" and I washed them and escorted them out to the Ballincollig direction. S. Mitchell and G. O'Brien and others used come to the house; catering much on the same scale as in Tan time. My work went on right up to the end. I carried ammunition from Greenmount to Pouladuff; I did less ammn. carrying in this time. Carried despatches 3 or 4 times. The house was a call-house for despatches.

## EVIDENCE OF T. CROFTS (SWORN) 24th Aug. 1945.

6. I knew the house in Pouladuff well; men stayed there. I couldn't say she carried guns. It was an extra good house. I can't say anything about her service after she got married but would presume she continued active.

## EVIDENCE OF MRS. MITCHELL (SWORN) 24th Aug. 1945.

9. In a round up in Sept. 1922 I went to her house for information about my husband's whereabouts. She came frequently in the following summer with food and coal for me and my children. They helped me generously.

## EVIDENCE OF JERM. O'BRIEN (SWORN) 24th Aug. 1945.

6. I was on the Intelligence staff of the Brigade in 1921 and she used do a lot for me - watching movements of agents around Pouladuff. She carried a grenade for me about May 1921 after an operation. I stayed in her house and so did members of the A.S.U. Her home in Pouladuff was used daily. I stayed there once a week.

7. I'd say on an average that men stayed in her house once a month. She was married in June 1920 (Mrs. Fennell) - the big numbers of men were kept in her parent's home.

                                             (P.T.O.)

Military records of Mamie. PG 78 A touch of Blarney.

**EVIDENCE OF MR. MOYNIHAN (SWORN) 24th August, 1945.**

4. I am an undertaker at Cobh.    Her husband was i/c. of that
Dept.;    the firm embalmed sailors;    he was able to get stuff
from the Yanks;    I saw him getting revolvers, I'd say 40 or 50
and ammunition. Mrs. Forde, even before she was married, used
come to the shop and he would give her stuff, I'd say 5 or 6
times.    This work went on for about 2 years from 1917.

**EVIDENCE OF SEÁN HEGARTY (SWORN) 24th Aug. 1945.**

6. She was a very good member of C. na mBan.    I don't think (but
I'm not sure) if she was in the house (her father's) when I
stayed there;    its Mrs. Fennell I mainly remember.    When I
visited the house I got it in a general way that they were very
good girls.    Her carrying of arms wasn't confined to the time
the Yanks were in Cobh.

- - - - - - - - - - - - - - - - - - - - - - - - - - - - - - - - - - - - - - - - - - -

**EVIDENCE OF SEÁN MITCHELL  24th January, 1946.**

6. During the Tan Period her husband was working in Cobh and he
7. was procuring bits of ammunition and an odd gun and he brought
them to Cork;    he was coffining Americans;    the wife collected
the stuff from his store in the city of Cork and brought it to
its destination.    She got married prior to the Tan War and had
rooms in the suburbs.    Her people were market gardeners and on
one or two occasions she took stuff out there to dump it.    Her
husband (a Vol.) got quite a lot of stuff.    I couldn't verify
that she brought stuff to Peter St. from Cobh.    She might bring
fellows out to the parents' home in Pouleduff but she wouldn't
be there herself.    I couldn't say that she kept men in
Greenmount.    She is a person I'd put before some who have
qualified.    I don't know many got pension.    If the Richardsons
got pensions, she is more deserving for hard-work.    She was
very helpful in taking out stuff to Pouleduff in case of raids.
I'd say she did more carrying of stuff than her husband;    I'd
say her estimate of 3 or 4 runs to Pouleduff is too low - 10
times would be more accurate.

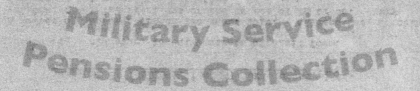

Military records of Mamie. PG 78 A touch of Blarney.

Rossduff Watford
27th April 1945

To whom it may concern

I beg to state that I know Mamie Forde for 30 years. I know her in the Cumn na mBan and can certify she was an exceptionally good worker in the movement from 1916 to 1922 and took a very active Part in helping the Volunteers at the time, in the way of taking Dispatches etc..

I also know her late Husband who was a member of the Volunteers from 1916 onwards as I was then capt. of the Company in the district Because of her activities in the Movement I consider Mrs Mamie Forde is intilled to a Cumn na mBan Pension.

Yours etc
J. Richardson
Formerly Capt D Company
Cork Brigade

Richardson Support letter. PG 78 A touch of Blarney.

Dear Sir,

This is to certify that Mr John Forde now [deceased] was in my employment for a number of years and had full charge of my Undertaking establishment during the period of the Great War. When we handled all the embalming of the American Sailors who lost their lives in our harbour and around our coast, We supplied them with lead-lined and lead coffins and this brought Mr Forde in close contact with the crews of the ships in the harbour who were in the position to give him the material he needed to help the old I.R.A. and I must say he availed of the opportunity.

I would like to add that his wife Mrs J. Forde was a very valuable asset in getting this material to its right destination. John Forde, as I knew him was a true and faithful servant to his Master and his country a good Irishman with a truly unselfish and God like Spirit and I firmly believe I can say the same of Mrs Forde. They both served their country well and there is no exaggeration in this statement.

Yours very respectfully
Stephen Moynihan. C.R.B.C.

Moynihans support letter. PG 30 American arrive in Cobh.

Cork Museum where Mamie's wedding dress and other millarty artefacts were lent.  Eileen (Mamie's daughter) and Noreen Dineen and Eillen OLeary (Mamies grandaughters). PG 79

# AFTON CIGARETTES

## *first for quality!*

M ........................................................................................

........................................................................................

........................19....

**JOHN J. HEGARTY,**
General Grocer,
Newsagent & Tobacconist,
**POULADUFF ROAD,**
Cork.

Phone: 238891

1960's bill head. PG 143 Liz & Shop.

### Medical Bills for Cork Explosion

On St Patrick's Day 1963, Gerry Madden survived the explosion at the Republican Plot in St Finbarr's Cemetery, Cork in which Desmond Swanton died. Madden was severely injured and lost an eye and his leg was amputated.

Dr Jack Barrett, General Surgeon at the Bon Secours Hospital tended Madden and Dr Jack Madden, Ophthalmic Surgeon dealt with the eye injury. The investigating police believed that they would identify the Republican faction from the bomb manufacture technique and they requested Dr Barrett to ask the patient what the device was made from. The patient said nothing. The surgeon said that it was a matter of indifference to him what kind of poisoning he chose to die to from, but if he wanted his care, then it would help to know what kind of metal still remained in the wound. "A Jacobs biscuit tin, sir".

Dr Barrett sent his account promptly to Thomas Ashe Hall and it was paid. Dr Madden was some time later when he tried to get paid by the same route. He was never paid. In those few months the sympathies of the persons in charge at the Hall may have changed.

This information was given by Dr Jack Barrett to Kieran Crowley, one of his in-laws. Dr Madden gave a similar account also to Kieran Crowley

_J. Kieran Crowley_

Kieran Crowley Letter. PG 157 New Republican plot.

In the latter part of the last century and the early part of the present when Ireland was in union with Britain the Irish representation at Westminister strove for the passing of legislation to give Home Rule to Ireland. A Home Rule Bill was passed in 1914 but it was suspended because of the War. However, the Insurrection of 1916 proclaimed that freedom was a God-given right and not something to be given out by a British Parliament. In 1918 a General Election was held and more than 75% of those elected to represent Ireland refused to go to Westminister. Instead, they met in Dublin, declared the Independence of the country at a meeting of the First Dail held on 21st January, 1919 (special stamp 21/1/69) and set up the machinery of government. The British Government did not accept the situation and continued to enforce its own rule by force of arms.

In this situation the Lord Mayor of Cork, Tomás MacCurtain, presided over a meeting of the Cork Corporation at which a resolution was passed declaring allegiance to the Dail. This set a pattern which, if followed by other local authorities would make the British position untenable. In consequence, MacCurtain was murdered on 19th March, 1920. The British authorities held an inquest and were amazed when the jury brought in a verdict of wilful murder against the British Government.

To succeed MacCurtain as Lord Mayor the Corporation elected his closest friend, Terence MacSwiney. On his election MacSwiney made an eloquent and moving speech declaring his determination to carry on the work of MacCurtain regardless of the personal consequences to him. On the 12th August the British military raided his office in the City Hall, took possession of his documents and arrested him. He was tried by courtmartial and sentenced to two years' imprisonment.

From the moment of his arrest MacSwiney refused to take any food. He was moved to Brixton prison and there, with the attention of the world focussed on him he died on 25th October after 75 days of fasting.

Although pressure to release MacSwiney was brought on the British from all quarters of the world, they adamantly refused and, at the same time increased their military measures to suppress the power and influence of the Dail. Guerilla warfare between the forces of the Dail (the I.R.A.) and Crown forces was now widespread. In one engagement in Dublin an I.R.A. youth aged 18 named Kevin Barry was captured. In an effort to get information about his comrades, Barry was tortured but he steadfastly refused to speak and, with a smile on his face, he walked to death on the gallows in Mountjoy Jail on the morning of the day on which Terence MacSwiney was buried in Cork beside his comrade Tomás MacCurtain.

Printed by Kellyprint Limited for the HARP COVER CLUB OF IRELAND, 110 Tyrconnell Park, Dublin 8.

An Post 50th Anniversary commemorative stamps. First Day of Issue Stamps - Oct 1970. PG 72/73 Terence McSweeney Lord Mayor of Cork.

John and Mamie on their Wedding Day (credit Barry's Photographers, Cork). PG 79

# Notes